TOPICS IN AUTISM

STOP that Seemingly Senseless Behavior!

FBA-BASED INTERVENTIONS FOR PEOPLE WITH AUTISM

Beth A. Glasberg, Ph.D., BCBA

Sandra L. Harris, Ph.D., series editor

Woodbine House ♦ 2008

© 2008 Beth A. Glasberg
First edition

All rights reserved under International and Pan American Copyright Conventions.
Published in the United States of America by Woodbine House, Inc., 6510 Bells Mill Rd.,
Bethesda, MD 20817. 800-843-7323. www.woodbinehouse.com

Library of Congress Cataloging-in-Publication Data

Glasberg, Beth A.
  Stop that seemingly senseless behavior! : FBA-based interventions for people with
autism / Beth A. Glasberg. -- 1st ed.
      p. cm. -- (Topics in autism)
  Includes bibliographical references and index.
  ISBN 978-1-890627-76-8
  1. Autism. 2. Behavioral assessment. I. Title.

RC553.A88G37 2008
616.85'882--dc22   2008037312

Manufactured in the United States of America

First Edition

10   9   8   7   6   5   4   3   2   1

*To individuals with autism
and their families everywhere*

Table of Contents

Introduction

Finally! That frustrating behavior problem—the one that previously seemed so senseless—is starting to make sense. Now that a functional behavior assessment (FBA) has been completed for your child or student, you can see how that "problem" behavior actually helps him improve his world. Now what? How can you use this information to ultimately make the problem disappear for good?

The short answer is that parents, teachers, and other caregivers must know not only how to identify the function of a behavior, but also how to use the information gathered during an FBA to produce behavior change. That is what this book will help you learn to do.

At this stage, maybe you will recognize your own concerns in the following stories.

Grace Carmichael

By October, Ms. Brandt was ready to quit her job. Although she had thoroughly enjoyed teaching her second grade class for the last several years, this year was different. Little Grace Carmichael was ruining her life. Grace was an eight-year-old girl with a pervasive developmental disorder (PDD) who was included in Ms. Brandt's general education classroom. Grace was very interested in other children and was excited to be in her new classroom and to have a chance to make new friends. Many days, Grace had no problems at all, but then suddenly she might pick up her chair and smash it on the foot of the child seated next to her. While doing a craft activity, she might bite a nearby student sitting on the arm. While standing in line, she might slap the child in front of her.

Ms. Brandt called in the school's behavior specialist, who found that Grace was using these behaviors to get her classmates' attention. Although Grace could speak well, she had trouble fitting in with the other children. She missed many of their nonverbal cues and often approached the wrong children at the wrong time, or the right children in the wrong way. Her aggressive behavior was actually the most efficient way for her to get a response from the other children. Meanwhile, Grace's difficulties with social skills prevented her from understanding that the response that she was getting for her aggression was worse than no response at all.

Although Ms. Brandt felt relieved that she now knew why Grace sometimes hurt other students, she still had no idea how to improve the situation enough so Grace could remain in her classroom.

Jamaal Brown's Story

Four-year-old Jamaal Brown had made wonderful progress in his home-based discrete trial instruction program. Not only was he flying through his academic, self-help, and motor programs, but he was also making excellent progress with social skills. He could have entire conversations about various topics while using appropriate body language and intonation. His parents and teachers were sure he was ready to interact with typically developing peers, and enrolled Jamaal in a children's gymnastics class to try it out.

Much to their dismay, Jamaal did not interact well with the other children. Although he watched them closely and seemed interested in their activities, he did not approach them. When peers approached him, Jamaal would look right at them while making a strange face and adopting a crooked posture with his body. Sadly, the other children quickly stopped trying to play with Jamaal. His parents and teachers were baffled. How was it that Jamaal's social skills inexplicably switched off when he was around other children?

Finally, Jamaal's teacher completed a functional behavior assessment for these problematic behaviors. He learned that Jamaal's behaviors scared off the other children, allowing Jamaal to escape the challenging task of peer interaction. How could the teachers get Jamaal the social skills practice with peers he desperately needed if he could so easily avoid interactions at will? After all, they couldn't force the other children to stay and interact with Jamaal.

Darra Littman

If Darra Littman's mother had told her once, she had told her a thousand times, no more discussion of pop singer Clay Aiken. Darra had seen Clay on the American Idol *television show and hadn't stopped talking about him since. She began to turn almost any conversation his direction, no matter how unrelated. These odd changes of topic made her peers uncomfortable and eventually resulted in them avoiding her. Nevertheless, Darra would discuss nothing else. Her mother forbade any discussion of Clay and made a rule that any mention of his name would cost Darra ten minutes of evening television time, which Darra treasured. Still, the "Clay talk" persisted. Even when Darra lost all two hours of her allotted television time, there was no discernable impact on the "Clay talk."*

Mrs. Littman asked Darra's school to complete a functional behavior assessment for this problem. The assessment revealed that Darra talked about Clay because it made her feel good, and that the loss of television time didn't decrease the "Clay talk" because Darra would rather talk about Clay than watch television anyway. Mrs. Littman thought, "Oh great! Now what am I supposed to do?"

Anthony Cappozolli

Mr. Cappozolli heard that familiar, unwelcome sound coming from the living room and went running. Just as he'd expected, he found Anthony, his nonverbal, fifteen-year-old son with autism, banging his head against the windowpane. "Anthony!" he yelled, pulling him away. He sternly reminded him that head banging is dangerous and not allowed. Mr. Cappozolli then led Anthony over to a box of beads, off limits at other times, that the family used to distract him from continuing this perilous behavior.

When Mr. Cappozolli hired a behavior analyst to help figure out why Anthony kept banging his head, she explained that head banging was actually Anthony's way of requesting the beads. This was the most efficient strategy he had to get them, and each time Mr. Cappozolli gave Anthony the beads to distract him from head banging, he was actually making the problem worse. Mr. Cappozolli felt helpless. What would he do the next time Anthony banged his head? He couldn't just let Anthony hurt himself or break the window, and Anthony was really too big to restrain.

Each of the above examples demonstrates that, while understanding a problem behavior is a critical first step in solving a behavior problem, understanding alone is unfortunately not enough. Behavior problems may be irritating or life-threatening, they may destroy property or relationships, or they may prevent an otherwise competent person from fully participating in the community. In any of these situations, the problem behavior needs to be stopped, and this can only occur if parents or teachers translate their understanding into action.

This book, a sequel to *Functional Behavior Assessment for People with Autism: Making Sense of Seemingly Senseless Behavior*, will help readers learn how to use information gathered during an FBA to produce positive behavioral change. Although this book reviews some of the basics of doing a functional behavior assessment (FBA), I assume that readers have read the previous book, or have otherwise acquired a working knowledge of the FBA process. This volume explains the next steps that should occur once an FBA has been completed. Specifically, readers will learn to use FBA results to develop informed, complete, and effective behavior intervention plans. A cornerstone of the Positive Behavior Support process (Carr, Horner, Turnbull, et al., 1999), plans based on FBAs allow interventionists to make specific changes to the environment to prevent or diminish problem behaviors.

Chapter 1 reviews the basics of FBA. It will serve to remind readers of the foundational concepts detailed in *Functional Behavior Assessment for People with Autism: Making Sense of Seemingly Senseless Behavior*. It summarizes strategies for identifying the function of a behavior, and explains why this helps lead to effective intervention. Chapter 2 provides an overview of learning theory with an eye toward helping readers understand how to help individuals "unlearn" problem behaviors.

Chapters 3 through 5 introduce general classes of intervention strategies. These strategies involve changing behavior by: 1) altering environmental variables in place before the problem behavior even occurs, 2) introducing new behaviors that can compete with the original problem behavior, or 3) changing how people respond to the problem behavior. Using these types of strategies, Chapter 6 demonstrates how to create specific behavior intervention packages suited for preventing or reducing behaviors that serve different functions.

Chapter 7 outlines ideas for adapting behavior intervention plans for special situations, such as addressing a problem behavior that serves multiple functions for an individual, or addressing behaviors in a group setting. Once a behavior plan is developed, Chapter 8 describes strategies to ensure that plans are implemented effectively. Specific support and formats for writing up behavior intervention plans are included in Chapter 9, while Chapter 10 offers help with managing unexpected behavior problems and other frequently asked questions. Finally, Chapter 11 discusses some strategies that may prevent individuals with autism spectrum disorders from developing challenging behaviors in the first place.

The aim of this book is to explain the above principles and strategies in plain English, so that parents and professionals can use them, together with the information gained through an FBA, to create sensible behavior interventions that will work. For readers who have the support of trained behavior analysts, this book will enable them to be more active participants in the process of creating and implementing behavior plans. Note that the strategies described here will not help to eliminate medically based problems such as tics. However, they will be useful in strategizing ways to make these medical issues less handicapping.

To achieve these goals, this book minimizes the use of jargon to the extent possible, offers practical suggestions, and uses "Keep it Simple" tips in each chapter to help readers manage complex concepts and use a step-by-step approach. Because communication and social skill deficits so commonly lead to problematic behaviors among individuals with autism and related disorders, this book will help parents, adult siblings, grandparents, group home staff, and other caregivers, as well as teachers, school psychologists, and other professionals who are concerned with individuals with autism spectrum disorders.

The methods described in this book can be used with toddlers, preschoolers, school-aged children, adolescents, and adults with any type of autism spectrum disorder, as well as other individuals with problem behaviors. Although this book focuses on autism spectrum disorders, it should be noted that most of the strategies described are equally useful for all people with developmental disabilities or other challenges who have problem behaviors.

In my work as a board certified behavior analyst, I have seen these strategies help hundreds of individuals with problem behaviors similar to those of Grace, Jamaal, Darra, and Anthony. I have also seen many parents, teachers, and others learn to apply them effectively. I hope that this book will provide the sensible intervention strategies needed to free someone you care about from a past that has created damaging, restrictive behaviors, and open the door to a more productive and inclusive future.

1 | Functional Behavior Assessment and Behavior Plans: An Overview

What Is an FBA and Why Should We Do It?

At first glance, most problem behaviors don't make sense. Think about Anthony inflicting pain on himself or Darra losing her television time (see the Introduction). Traditional interventions did not work for these youngsters because the people creating the interventions couldn't make sense of what was happening. This is where functional behavior assessment (FBA) comes into play. FBA describes a systematic set of scientific procedures designed to obtain information and develop hypotheses about the purposes (functions) a behavior serves for a person.

As discussed in the Introduction to this book and in *Functional Behavior Assessment for People with Autism: Making Sense of Seemingly Senseless Behavior*, behaviors that seem completely senseless to onlookers actually make sense for the person engaging in the behavior. That is why these frustrating behaviors persist. If there were a more efficient way for Anthony or Darra to get what they wanted, then they would do that instead. Functional behavior assessment is the set of procedures that we use to identify what the person actually wants, and what is going on in his environment that makes the problem behavior the best way to get it. We call this new understanding of the behavior the "function" of the behavior. It answers the question, how does this behavior "function" in the individual's environment?

Ted Carr and Mark Durand (1985) were the first to document predictable relationships between problem behaviors and an individual's environment. They demonstrated that some of the people in their study only displayed problem behaviors when they were receiving very little attention, while others only displayed problem behaviors when they were given a very difficult task to do. Each individual showed his own unique relationship between the problem behavior and what was going on in the environment.

Many researchers have now shown that systematically studying the reasons behind a problem behavior can lead to an effective intervention for that behavior. Specifically, research has clearly demonstrated that intervention plans based on the results of an FBA are more likely to be effective than plans based on trial and error (e.g., Repp, Felce, & Barton, 1988).

The science behind functional behavior assessment is so compelling that, legally, public schools in the United States *must* consider completing an FBA when addressing challenging behaviors in a student with disabilities (Individuals with Disabilities Education Act, 2004). Study after study shows that relying on a thorough functional behavior assessment is the most likely way to succeed in reducing or eliminating an unwanted behavior (e.g., Iwata et al., 1994). Behavior intervention plans based on functional behavior assessments work for individuals of all ages and all functioning levels (e.g., Austin, Weatherly, & Gravina, 2005; Ervin, DuPaul, Kern, & Friman, 1998).

Why FBA Is More Effective Than Trial and Error

Not only are interventions based on an FBA more likely to be effective, they are more likely to be effective the first time. With a trial and error approach, one intervention after another is created, implemented, and allowed time for its effectiveness to be evaluated. All the while, the individual's problem behavior is persisting at best, and growing more severe at worst. Although doing an FBA requires an investment of time early in the process, it is likely to result in a quicker reduction in the problem behavior in the long run.

Furthermore, an intervention based on a functional assessment may help prevent or reduce future problem behavior. For example, consider Anthony from the Introduction. Once we have determined that his head-banging is a way of requesting beads, we are alerted to the fact that Anthony needs help making requests in general. We may help Anthony build a broad repertoire of requests as part of the intervention. This, in turn, decreases his need to bang his head to obtain desired items in the future.

Anthony's case story highlights one of the most important features of a functionally based approach: It is educational. Interventions based on an FBA leave the individual with increased skills, capabilities, and options. For people with autism spectrum disorders who may be challenged in their communication and social skills, FBA may provide essential information that leads to an improved quality of life.

Understanding the function of a problem behavior can prevent parents and professionals from taking a misstep. For example, using a trial-and-error approach, a parent or teacher might decide to use Time Out (removing the child from the situation) whenever the child begins to bite himself. But when Brian Iwata and his colleagues (1994) reviewed data on over 150 people with a history of self-injurious behavior, they found that many of them used the behavior to escape or avoid something. If Time-Out is used as a consequence for a behavior that the person uses to escape a situation, then we are inadvertently teaching the student to perform the problem behavior. Think about it: The child wants to escape, so he launches into the problem behavior, and he is given a Time-Out (escape). This teaches the child that the problem behavior leads to escape. When the child wants to escape something, he will simply engage in the problem behavior again.

Consider another trial-and-error intervention approach commonly used. Let's say that Robert, a nonverbal adult with autism living in a group home, hates putting dishes away. He discovers that if he breaks a dish on the kitchen floor, someone else takes over the task and he is no longer trusted to put the rest of the dishes away. To discourage this behavior, the group home staff may decide to use an "overcorrection" and have Robert clean not only the broken dishes, but the whole kitchen floor. This may, in fact, stop Robert from breaking dishes. However, he still has no way to communicate that he does not like putting dishes away (or that he does not like some other task). He may come up with a different way to escape tasks that may be no more desirable, or even less desirable, than breaking dishes. Although Robert is no longer breaking dishes, the problem is still not solved, as he still has no adaptive way to get his needs met.

What Are the Possible Functions of a Problem Behavior?

You might think there would be an infinite number of purposes for engaging in a challenging behavior, but years of research have shown that we can describe all of these different motivations according to one of four general categories of "functions." Although different professionals characterize these possible functions in slightly different ways, these different systems are equivalent to one another (e.g., Iwata, et al., 1994; Durand & Crimmins, 1992). This book will characterize the four possible functions of behavior as follows:

1. **Attention.** The behavior is motivated by the person's desire to receive attention from one or more people. The desired attention can be of varying qualities. For example, the person might want vocal or physical attention, low-key or intense attention, or attention from one person or a group of people. Grace's aggressive behavior, described in the Introduction, exemplifies this type of function. She was behaving aggressively toward her classmates in order to get their attention, even though it was not good quality, positive attention.

2. **Objects and activities.** An individual may use behavior to gain access to any desired object or activity, such as food, drink, toys, privileges, etc. Anthony's problem behavior, described in the Introduction, exemplifies this type of function. Anthony used head-banging as a means to request his beads.

3. **Escape/avoid.** Behaviors that are motivated by this function help someone to escape or avoid a task, or anything that he perceives to be aversive. Jamaal's problem behavior, from the Introduction, exemplifies this type of function. His odd facial expressions and body postures kept the other children in gym class from interacting with him.

4. **Automatic reinforcement.** These types of behaviors are repeated because they feel good, alleviate pain, or otherwise lead to reinforcing internal stimulation for an individual. Darra's behavior, from the Introduction, exemplifies this type of function. For some reason, she

found talking about Clay Aiken intrinsically satisfying, regardless of others' reactions to her monologues.

Combinations of functions are also possible. That is, one behavior can serve more than one function. For example, if a student hits a classmate, this might result in removal from the classroom (escape) as well as a talk with the guidance counselor (attention). When one behavior serves more than one function, it is called a "multi-operant" behavior. Multi-operant behaviors are especially common among people with limited communication abilities, as problem behaviors may be the most efficient way for them to control their environment. Multi-operant behaviors are also common in less flexible environments where an individual's requests may be ignored even if he makes it appropriately.

Additionally, a child or adult can use multiple behaviors to serve the same function. For example, a student might raise his hand, call out, and make wisecracks, all to obtain teacher attention. Which behavior a child chooses at a given time will depend on changing variables in his environment (to be discussed in Chapter 2). When people receive less consistent responses to their appropriate and inappropriate behaviors, they are likely to develop a wider repertoire of strategies to get their needs met.

Getting Started

The first step in developing a behavior intervention plan is to determine whether or not an intervention is needed. This involves collecting "baseline" data about the current frequency and intensity of the behavior to see how much of a problem it presents for the individual and people in his environment. (See the book, *Functional Assessment for People with Autism: Making Sense of Seemingly Senseless Behaviors,* for detailed information on collecting and using "baseline" data.)

In summary, a behavior merits intervention if:
- It presents a danger to the individual or others;
- It is leading to destruction of property; or
- It is interfering with the individual's ability to get access to the objects and activities he prefers.

In addition, the behavior must be:

- occurring at a high enough level to cause significant impairment,
- either remaining at a high level or increasing, and
- fairly stable.

Following these guidelines to choose behaviors to target will ensure that you do not unnecessarily restrict the person's independence or unnecessarily expend valuable resources.

How Can I Tell Which Function a Behavior Serves?

There are a number of procedures that can help us identify the function of a specific behavior. Generally speaking, every FBA must include observation, interview, and descriptive assessment. Some hypothesis testing or demonstration of experimental control is also desirable. Each of these steps is described briefly below. For more detailed information, forms, and procedures, see *Functional Behavior Assessment for People with Autism: Making Sense of Seemingly Senseless Behavior.*

Observation

Observation of the person who is engaging in the problem behavior—both during the behavior and when the behavior is not occurring—is an essential first step. It allows the intervention team to begin to notice whether the individual's environment changes before and after the problem behavior, and if so, how.

For example, consider Nick, a student who is returning to the classroom from a break, about to engage in his school work. If Nick flops down on the floor and is then taken out of his classroom to receive sensory input (a common intervention for students with autism)—how has his behavior changed the environment? Before Nick's flopping behavior, it was time for work. After the behavior, it was time for sensory input. Now Nick has likely learned that flopping on the floor is a good way to escape from work.

Let's consider this example further. Are there times when Nick does *not* flop on the floor before he is asked to work? If we discover that he only flops on the way to table work, but not on the way to group work or work in the media center, art room, or gym, we can assume that something about his table work needs to be changed to better suit his needs. The work may be too hard, or too easy. It may involve nonpreferred materials, or nonpreferred subjects. It might be too repetitive, or too meaningless. In any case, part of the assessment will be to pinpoint the exact problem associated with the table work and to figure out how to resolve that problem.

In continuing our observation, we can note which environmental supports are in place when the individual engages in the problem behavior, as opposed to when he chooses not to engage in the behavior. We can also see how people respond to the problem behavior, and compare this to how they respond to the individual's appropriate requests.

Interview

We cannot observe someone in every possible setting. Therefore, we must also interview significant others about the person's behavior and include their information in our assessment.

During the interview, we investigate the same basic question as during an observation: In what way is the problem behavior helping the individual to control his environment? We ask about:

- when the behavior is more or less likely to occur;
- what skills the individual has to get his needs met appropriately;
- whether or not there are situations where the individual is guaranteed to use or not use the behavior;
- what happens before and after the behavior.

These are just a few examples of interview questions that might be helpful. Be sure to interview multiple people who see the individual in a variety of settings.

Don't be surprised if the responses from different interviewees do not match. Sometimes, consequences for behaviors are different in different environments, which lead to different behavior patterns in different settings. For example, Mom may find it easy to ignore her child's pleading for extra cookies and the behavior may disappear at home very quickly. In contrast, Grandma may find it hard to refuse a pleading child. As a result, the pleading might be much more likely to occur at Grandma's house. Another reason that interviewees' responses may not match is that sometimes people simply disagree.

Descriptive Assessment

Descriptive assessments quantify the environment and events surrounding the behavior. One popular form of descriptive assessment is collecting "ABC" (Antecedent-Behavior-Consequence) data. This type of data collection centers on documenting what occurs immediately before and after the problem behavior. This allows you to search for patterns. For example, whenever Mom gets on the phone, little Johnny hits his sister, resulting in Mom hanging up the phone and returning her attention to Johnny.

ABC data can be taken in a narrative format (just writing down what has occurred), or in a checklist created for a specific response which may or may not address specific hypotheses. For example, Figure 1 shows a checklist designed to find out what prompts a particular student's problem behaviors of screaming and running away.

Another type of descriptive assessment involves documenting how often the problem behavior occurs under different environmental conditions. For example, how often does the behavior occur when the individual is asked to perform a task? How often does the behavior occur when the individual has very little attention? Figure 2 on page 10 provides an example of a chart designed to collect this type of descriptive data for a behavior that an individual uses to obtain desired items.

Hypothesis Testing

Sometimes, observation, interview, and descriptive assessment corroborate one another and the intervention team feels confident that they understand the function of the behavior. However, sometimes, after preliminary assessments, the team remains confused. In this case, more scientific "hypothesis testing" is required. Additionally, hypothesis testing is good practice to ensure a correct assessment even if the team is fairly confident of its findings.

During hypothesis testing, the intervention team seeks to demonstrate "prediction and control" over the problem behavior. This means that team members can predict the conditions under which a behavior is likely to occur, create those conditions, and actually make the behavior occur. Conversely, the team can demonstrate that the behavior will not occur under different conditions. For example, imagine that

Figure 1 | Sample ABC Checklist

What happened JUST before the problem behavior?	What was the behavior?	What happened JUST after the problem behavior?	Did behavior immediately stop?
❑ given an instruction ❑ approached by peer ❑ teacher turned to work with another student ❑ other	❑ screamed ❑ ran away	❑ chased ❑ prompted to complete task ❑ prompted to reply to peer ❑ redirected to new activity ❑ other	❑ yes ❑ no
❑ given an instruction ❑ approached by peer ❑ teacher turned to work with another student ❑ other	❑ screamed ❑ ran away	❑ chased ❑ prompted to complete task ❑ prompted to reply to peer ❑ redirected to new activity ❑ other	❑ yes ❑ no
❑ given an instruction ❑ approached by peer ❑ teacher turned to work with another student ❑ other	❑ screamed ❑ ran away	❑ chased ❑ prompted to complete task ❑ prompted to reply to peer ❑ redirected to new activity ❑ other	❑ yes ❑ no
❑ given an instruction ❑ approached by peer ❑ teacher turned to work with another student ❑ other	❑ screamed ❑ ran away	❑ chased ❑ prompted to complete task ❑ prompted to reply to peer ❑ redirected to new activity ❑ other	❑ yes ❑ no
❑ given an instruction ❑ approached by peer ❑ teacher turned to work with another student ❑ other	❑ screamed ❑ ran away	❑ chased ❑ prompted to complete task ❑ prompted to reply to peer ❑ redirected to new activity ❑ other	❑ yes ❑ no

Figure 2	Descriptive Analysis Checklist		
Definition of behavior:	Mark this column if a demand was in place at the time of the problem behavior.	Mark this column if there was no attention being given to the individual at the time of the problem behavior.	Mark this column if the individual wanted something he or she could not have at the time of the problem behavior.
Incident 1			
Incident 2			
Incident 3			
Incident 4			
Incident 5			
Incident 6			
Incident 7			
Incident 8			
Incident 9			
Incident 10			
Incident 11			
Incident 12			
Incident 13			
Incident 14			
Incident 15			

Grace's assessment team predicts that she will hit peers only when she is not already receiving attention from a peer. The team will test this prediction by having a classmate play with Grace for 15 minutes and counting the number of aggression attempts. Then they will instruct the child not to play with Grace for 15 minutes and will count Grace's aggression attempts.

When using hypothesis testing, each condition is repeated at least two or three times to ensure that the data are consistent over time. Repeated patterns of high rates of behavior in one condition and low rates in another suggest that the behavior is functioning on the environment in a predictable way.

Functional Analysis

For especially confusing behaviors, you may need to use a more systematic approach to isolating the antecedents and consequences in order to identify the function of the behavior. This very controlled and scientific approach to assessment, referred to as functional analysis, involves actually reinforcing the problem behavior. For example, to determine whether or not Samantha is biting to obtain adult attention, she might be placed in a room alone with an adult. The adult will explain that she needs to do something right now and will play with Samantha after she is done with her task. Then, the adult will ignore Samantha. If Samantha bites her to get her attention, she will pay attention to her briefly (e.g., 30 seconds) and then return to her "work."

Although this approach may sound strange and counterintuitive, it replicates what might be happening inadvertently in the natural environment. If, in fact, Samantha is using biting to obtain attention, we should see her biting increase over repeated sessions of this type. Samantha will recognize the pattern of antecedents and consequences. In contrast, if Samantha is actually biting to obtain access to a preferred item (e.g., she is only given a binky or pacifier when she bites), she will not continue to bite when she is provided with attention after each bite. She doesn't want attention, so she will learn from experiencing the pattern of cues and consequences that biting doesn't work to get her binky in this setting.

Functional analysis involves multiple sessions over time. During those sessions, team members document the function of the behavior

Keep It Simple Summary

- Understanding the function of a problem behavior improves our chances of successfully eliminating it.
- There are four general types of functions of behavior:
    1. obtaining attention,
    2. escaping or avoiding a demanding situation,
    3. obtaining access to desired items or activities,
    4. automatic reinforcement.
- By using established FBA procedures, an intervention team can identify the function or functions that a behavior serves.

by actually getting the individual to increase the behavior over time. As you might imagine, multiple staff members are needed in order to control the necessary environmental variables, record the relevant data, and keep all participants safe. Therefore, this approach should only be conducted under the guidance of an experienced behavior analyst.

2 | How Are Behaviors Unlearned?

Chapter 1 reminds us that the problem behaviors of our children, students, and clients have all been learned from their experiences, although these are lessons that we did not intend to teach! There is nothing magical or irrational about these behavior problems; they are simply a product of learning. That is why our FBAs empower us. Once we know the function or functions of a behavior and how it has been learned, we can change things around so that the behavior is "unlearned." In this chapter, we will review the basic process of learning with an eye toward intervention based on unlearning.

This will be the most technical section of the book. However, once you have the following basic behavioral concepts under your belt, you will be armed and ready to learn specific strategies to un-teach anything that your child, student, or client needs to unlearn!

Overview of Learning (and Unlearning) Theory

Learning implies that a behavior is added to an individual's repertoire in a relatively permanent way. Unlearning, then, implies removing a behavior from an individual's repertoire. That is what we are trying to do. In order to understand the best ways to help someone unlearn a behavior, we must first understand the basic principles of learning. Learning (and therefore unlearning) occurs as part of a four-part equation:

Motivation → Antecedent + Behavior + Consequence

Each component of the learning equation will be explained below.

1. Motivation

Learning and unlearning begin with motivation. Motivation, in everyday language, refers to what a person wants or desires, as well as how hard he or she is willing to work to get it. For example, a teacher might be motivated to get rid of a student's challenging behavior, or motivated to earn tenure, or motivated to be assigned as a department head.

In the study of behavior, the meaning of motivation is very close to this, but we think of motivation only in terms of external, measurable factors. For example, while "hunger" is not quantifiable (a nonbehavioral description), the number of hours since the last meal can be easily measured (a behavioral understanding of motivation for food). Because motivation drives behavior, when we change the environment in ways that change motivators (the conditions or things that motivate behavior), we ultimately change behavior. For example, if we give food to a child who hasn't eaten for five hours, she will decrease behaviors that are geared toward obtaining food.

Measuring Motivation: Establishing Operations

In behavior analysis, motivation has historically been described according to a quantifiable process referred to as an "establishing operation" or "EO" (Michael, 1982). In simplest terms, the establishing operation is what makes something a reinforcer for somebody at any given moment. (It is something that "operates" on someone's environment and "establishes" a motivation for certain items or events.) Continuing the example above, the length of time since the last meal can be considered an EO for food. The longer someone goes without food (and the hungrier she gets), the more motivated she usually is to try to obtain some food.

Establishing operations cause us to try behaviors that have worked in the past to get the things that we want. Continuing our example, food deprivation may cause us to make requests for food or take trips to the refrigerator, if we have successfully used those behaviors in the past to obtain food.

Thinking about EOs highlights the ever-changing nature of motivators. For example, every minute since a meal, the motivation for food grows stronger. Conversely, every bite that is consumed decreases the motivation to seek out additional food. The EO is in constant flux, and therefore, so is the value of food to the individual. How many times have you thought, "I can't believe my student is not working for this food reward; it is her favorite!" But favorite foods will only motivate a child to use the behaviors we want when she is in a state of deprivation (having had too little). If she has had too much (satiation) the "favorite" will not motivate her. If the child had access to the favored item periodically all day long (and has reached satiation), she will no longer value further access to it. In contrast, if the child hasn't had access to that favored item all week (deprivation), then she will probably be willing to work very hard to get it.

Measuring Changes in Motivation: Motivating and Abolishing Operations

Relatively recently, experts in motivation have pointed out that EO really only describes events that increase an individual's motivation to do certain behaviors. They felt that we also need a way to describe environmental events that decrease an individual's motivation to do certain behaviors. As a result, leading behavior analysts in the field of motivation have recommended a change in terms (Laraway, Snycerski, Michael, & Poling, 2001). These new terms are intended to clarify the varying effects an environmental change may have on motivation. Therefore, the less specific term EO has been replaced by two different terms:

1. Motivating Operations (MOs), and
2. Abolishing Operations (AOs)

"**Motivating Operations**" or "MOs" refer to changes in the environment that: 1) increase the value of an item or event to a person at a given moment, and 2) increase the efforts and actions that the person will take in order to gain access to that item or event. For example, lowering the temperature in a house increases the value of obtaining a sweater. It will also lead to behaviors that have resulted in obtaining a sweater in the past, such as going to the closet.

In contrast, when an environmental event: 1) decreases the value of an item or activity to a person at a given moment, and 2) decreases the efforts and actions the person will take to obtain it, it is called an "**Abolishing Operation**" or "AO." Following our earlier example, raising the temperature in the house decreases the value of obtaining a sweater, and decreases the chances that someone will go to their closet to get one.

MO and AO in Action

The story of 13-year-old Amos's FBA illustrates why it is important to understand an individual's MO and AO:

Amos had recently and inexplicably become more aggressive. Specifically, he was hitting teachers hard enough to leave bruises and pinching them hard enough to leave little welts. Given his recent growth spurt, and the fact that he was now bigger than most of his teachers, this aggressive behavior was particularly unsafe and difficult to manage. Observation, interview, and descriptive assessments had not clarified the function of his aggression. The team decided that some more systematic hypothesis testing sessions would be needed to help them understand what Amos had learned about using aggressive behaviors.

At first, because Amos's behaviors were severe, the team agreed on five-minute test sessions. During these sessions, the team carefully controlled possible contributing variables so they could isolate one potential function at a time. Based on observation, interview, and descriptive assessment, the following hypotheses were tested:

Hypotheses about the Function of Amos's Aggression

Comparison Condition (to serve as a control condition for other test conditions)	Amos rests on the couch with no demands, an attentive instructor nearby, and free access to preferred items/activities.
Divided Attention (Does it bother Amos when he doesn't get an adult's undivided attention?)	While Amos rests on the couch with no demands and free access to preferred items/activities, a second adult comes over and chats with his one-to-one instructor.
Restricted Access (Does it bother Amos when he can't get his favorite items whenever he wants them?)	Amos rests on the couch with no demands and an attentive instructor nearby. After a brief period of access to one of his favorite things, the item is placed in view but off-limits to Amos.

After two days of multiple, five-minute sessions, Amos had not engaged in any inappropriate behaviors. The team suspected that this amount of time was not long enough to elicit the problem behaviors. In other words, five minutes of depriving Amos of his preferred items or undivided attention did not leave him motivated enough to exert himself to obtain the desired consequence. A behavior analyst would say that the Motivating Operation (MO) was too weak at that point. To test this, the team increased the length of the sessions to 15 minutes. Something very interesting then occurred. In the control and divided attention conditions, Amos still had no challenging behaviors and made no attempts to get more attention. However, the data during sessions when his access to favorite items was restricted consistently looked like this:

- Minutes 1-5: No challenging behaviors or attempts
- Minutes 6-10: Unsuccessful swats at the teacher who was out of arm's reach
- Minutes 11-15: Amos gets up and hits or pinches teacher repeatedly

These data clearly illustrate the control of an MO over Amos's behavior. As the MO got stronger (due to longer periods of deprivation from a preferred item), Amos was willing to exert greater and greater effort to get what he wanted. After a few sessions had demonstrated this pattern, the teacher was asked to stay within arm's reach of Amos. Sure enough, the aggression then began around minute six.

This assessment process helped us to understand that Amos had learned to use aggression to request preferred items and activities in response to an MO for these rewards. Because his behaviors had grown so dangerous, we needed to immediately change the environment in such a way that Amos would be less likely to use the aggressive behaviors. In other words, we needed to create an Abolishing Operation (AO). The strategies we put in place to this end did not constitute his whole intervention package, which would take more time to describe. Instead, these were first steps toward a plan, and a crisis management strategy to keep everyone safe while a plan was developed.

First of all, Amos was given free access to his preferred items, regardless of his behavior in the interim, every 10 minutes. We had learned from our assessment that the MO was not strong enough at 10 minutes to get him up off the couch. Furthermore, after Amos had access to these items every 10 minutes all day, they would become less valuable to him. Next, we asked the instructors to stay out of arm's reach of Amos. We had learned from our assessment that if Amos needed to make a greater effort to behave aggressively (like standing up), he was less likely to try to hit his teachers. Together, these strategies created an AO for hitting that kept the teachers safe while a more thorough plan could be created.

As we can see from our example, everyone can typically tolerate a certain strength of an MO before they feel compelled to respond.

Usually, that strength is relatively consistent. For Amos, the breaking point for hitting when he was unable to obtain his preferred items was roughly six minutes. You may have seen other illustrations of this principle in your own experience. For example, many teachers have encountered students who engage in challenging behaviors when they are in groups. Typically, the student behaves appropriately in the group for a certain amount of time and then starts the problem behaviors. Similarly, you may have experienced this principle firsthand if you have ever tried to stay on a diet. You might resist preferred treats for roughly the same amount of time every day before giving in. (I, personally, usually stay on my diets until about dinner time.) You can think of the average strength of the MO that elicits the problem behavior as the "threshold" of what that individual can tolerate.

You may also notice that there are days that your child, students, or clients have a "shorter fuse." For example, many teachers have told me that they can tell by their student's face in the morning what kind of a day it will be. What these teachers are noticing is that on certain days, the student's threshold for certain behaviors has been changed. Less deprivation or satiation than usual will be required to elicit the problem behavior. This change in threshold happens in response to a "setting event" (Kantor, 1959).

A setting event can be thought of as something that happens well in advance of a behavior that alters the threshold for the MO that leads to the behavior. By changing the threshold that will lead to the behavior, setting events make behaviors more or less likely to occur. For example, if a child doesn't get a good night's sleep, she may not be able to wait as

Keep It Simple Summary

1. **MOs (Motivating Operations)** are environmental changes that increase the value of a certain outcome for a person, and elicit behaviors that have led to the person obtaining that outcome in the past.

2. **AOs (Abolishing Operations)** are environmental changes that decrease the value of a certain outcome for a person, and suppress behaviors that have led to the person obtaining that outcome in the past.

3. **Setting events** may occur far in advance of a specific behavior yet continue to affect the likelihood that it will occur.

long as usual for things that she wants—i.e., she has a lower threshold for waiting. We have all probably "pushed the limit" with our children or students for a special occasion—for instance, by letting them stay up late for fireworks or for a sibling's sleep-over party. Then the next day, we pay the price by getting tantrum after tantrum just because a waffle is taking too long to cook, or something of that nature. We quickly learn that lack of sleep might give our child a "shorter fuse." Similarly, if an adult who is addicted to coffee does not get her coffee in the morning, it may alter her behavior throughout the day.

2. *Antecedents*

The next variable in the learning equation is the immediate antecedent to a behavior. Broadly speaking, an antecedent is whatever changes in the environment the moment before a behavior occurs. For example, in our introduction, we met Jamaal, who makes odd faces and adopts unusual postures whenever other children try to interact with him. In this example, what the peer says or does is the immediate antecedent to Jamaal's behavior.

There are different types of antecedents that are important in learning and unlearning. The first type of antecedent acts as a cue that a desired outcome is available for performing a certain behavior, and actually elicits that behavior. For example, when Jamaal sees a peer, he has learned that he can escape interaction (a desired outcome) if he uses odd postures, and so he makes those postures. The technical name for this type of antecedent is a **discriminative stimulus** or S^D.

Because we are interested in the role that unlearning plays in behavioral change, two other types of antecedent variables are important to us. The first is an antecedent that has been associated with punishment for a certain behavior. For example, one teacher may respond to Jamaal's posturing by having him repeatedly practice appropriate interactions (i.e., more interaction, rather than less, as a consequence for posturing). If so, Jamaal will be less likely to use his postures in this teacher's presence. This type of antecedent is called a **punishing stimulus** or S^P.

There are also people and things in the environment that a given individual will not have learned to associate with either desired or undesired outcomes. These are events that the person has not learned to pair with meaningful consequences. For example, Jamaal may not have learned anything about seagulls, and so may not engage in any specific behavior when he sees one nearby. The technical term for this type of stimulus that is not associated with the challenging behavior is **stimulus delta** or $S^\triangle$.

Each of these three types of stimuli acquires its power over the behavior of any given person when that person consistently links the antecedent stimulus, a certain behavior, and a specific outcome. The key for unlearning behaviors is to break the patterns that have historically occurred and introduce the person to new, more adaptive patterns. For example, the children in Jamaal's class might be taught to respond to Jamaal's posturing with a hug or friendly chat. Then Jamaal would no longer link posturing with being able to escape from peer interaction. As a consequence, he might not make odd postures when his peers approach. However, this intervention would not be sufficient to change Jamaal's behavior, since his motivation to escape peer interaction has not been addressed, and he has not been taught a more appropriate means of getting out of interactions. Jamaal would therefore be likely to discover a new (but not necessarily a desirable) means of escape.

Keep It Simple Summary

Antecedents are events that occur just before a behavior. There are three types:

1. an antecedent that cues an individual that a certain behavior will be reinforced—a discriminative stimulus (S^D);
2. an antecedent that cues an individual that a certain behavior will be punished—a punishing stimulus (S^P);
3. an antecedent that has not consistently paired a behavior with reinforcement or punishment in the past—a stimulus delta ($S^\triangle$).

3. Behavior

A behavior is whatever an individual is doing. Examples include: eating too many desserts or head banging. Those are problematic behaviors that we want to decrease. However, there are also an infinite number of adaptive or helpful behaviors, such as exercising or asking for things that we want. When we use FBA results to design interventions for problem behaviors, we always include teaching "replacement" behaviors as part of the plan. Replacement behaviors are adaptive behaviors that serve the same purpose as the targeted problem behaviors. In other words, replacement behaviors give an individual an appropriate way to get her needs met.

Behavior analysts use the "Fair Pair" rule to ensure that they develop a sensible intervention (White & Haring, 1980). The Fair Pair rule states that for every behavior that we aim to decrease, we must aim to increase another. Typically, the behavior we aim to increase is the replacement skill. When we choose a replacement skill and arrange the environment in such a way that the replacement behavior is more efficient for someone than a problem behavior, we make the problem behavior obsolete. Chapter 4 discusses specific strategies related to identifying potentially effective replacement behaviors and ensuring their success.

Keep It Simple Summary

- A behavior is anything that a person does.
- A replacement behavior is a more appropriate behavior that accomplishes the same function as the problem behavior.

4. Consequences

A consequence is what occurs as the result of a behavior. In general, a consequence can be:

1. reinforcement, or
2. punishment.

Reinforcement

Reinforcement involves consequences that "strengthen" behavior, either by increasing the likelihood that it will occur in the future, or by increasing its intensity or duration in the future. Examples of reinforcement include telling your daughter that a dress looks good on her, resulting in her wearing that dress very often; or giving a child a quarter for cleaning her room, resulting in her cleaning it every day.

There are two types of reinforcement procedures: positive reinforcement and negative reinforcement. **Positive reinforcement** involves strengthening a behavior by adding something to the individual's environment in response to that behavior. For example, in the case story given in the Introduction, beads were added to Anthony's environment as a consequence for head banging. **Negative reinforcement** involves strengthening a behavior by removing something from someone's environment in response to that behavior. For example, Jamaal escaped peer interactions (removed the peers) as a consequence of making odd postures.

The only way to determine whether a given consequence is a reinforcer is to measure its effect on behavior. If it increases a behavior, it's a reinforcer. If it decreases a behavior or fails to affect it, it's not a reinforcer. Reinforcers do not always look appealing to outsiders, but if they strengthen behaviors, they are reinforcers nonetheless.

Using Reinforcement to Unlearn Behavior. There are three general ways to use reinforcement to help people unlearn behaviors. You can use one or more of these strategies. A brief introduction to each follows below, and a more detailed discussion of these strategies is provided in Chapter 5.

1. **Stop reinforcing the problem behavior.** When a behavior that was previously reinforced ceases to result in reinforcement, the behavior will undergo "extinction." In other words, the response will gradually disappear from an individual's repertoire. In some cases, you may see an "extinction burst." This refers to a sudden increase in the frequency or intensity of the behavior before it disappears. You may also see a sudden increase in related behaviors. For example, imagine if you picked up the telephone receiver in your house and there was no dial tone (the expected reinforcer). Your first response may be to simply hang the phone up and try again, but you may progress to pressing random buttons, checking the wire, hitting the phone, slamming it down, hanging it up repeatedly, etc. These responses would characterize an "extinction burst." Eventually, however, you would give up and walk away from the phone. At that point, your phone-checking behaviors are extinct.

2. **Differentially reinforce a replacement skill.** The extinction burst example described above is not harmful or

dangerous to anyone. However, the behaviors that have prompted you to read this book might be. For example, if Anthony is banging his head against a window, that alone is too dangerous to tolerate. We certainly could not simply stop giving Anthony the beads that he is using head banging to request. That is, we cannot use extinction on his head banging, given that it might cause the behavior to initially escalate.

For behaviors that are too dangerous for extinction, we will actually continue to reinforce the behavior. This might be the only way to stop the behavior in the moment. However, we will provide only the lowest level of reinforcement that will work. In contrast, we will provide high, intense levels of the reinforcer for an alternative, appropriate behavior. This should make the practice of the alternative behavior more enticing than the challenging behavior. For example, if Anthony bangs his head, we could give him five or six beads to play with. If, on the other hand, he requests beads with a picture card, we could give him a big box of hundreds of brightly colored beads.

3. **Deliver the reinforcer noncontingently.** In order to act as a reinforcer, the desired consequence must occur contingent upon (uniquely as a consequence of) a specific behavior. Otherwise, the relationship between the problem behavior and the reinforcing consequence will be broken. For example, if you could receive your paycheck for doing something other than going to work, you might skip work sometimes.

A common, yet misguided, strategy often used by parents of young children provides another good example. Young children will sometimes scream to request what they want. Intending to teach more appropriate behavior, a parent often says something like, "Use your friendly voice to ask." When the child repeats the request in a friendly voice, the parent delivers the desired item (reinforcer). However, if the child makes the same request appropriately the first time, her parent might not give her what she wants. It is only being reinforced as part of the parent's well-meaning plan to teach the use of a friendly voice. But, what has the contingency been?

    a. Ask nicely, no reinforcer.

    b. Scream first, get prompted to ask nicely, ask nicely, get a reinforcer.

The child has learned that reinforcement is contingent upon a "chain," or sequence, of screaming, getting prompted, and then asking nicely. This contingency can be broken by sometimes giving the child desired items when she does not request them, sometimes giving her the items in response to asking nicely the first time, and sometimes delivering the reinforcer after she first screams. By breaking the contingency between screaming and getting the reinforcer, screaming becomes unnecessary, and the child unlearns the "scream-first" response.

Punishment

A second type of consequence that might follow a behavior is punishment. A punisher is any consequence that decreases the strength (future probability, intensity, or duration) of a behavior. An example of a punisher is your dinner guest telling you, in a lukewarm tone, that the elaborate meal you worked so hard to prepare tastes "fine." The future probability of your preparing that meal again will surely decrease.

Like reinforcement, punishment is defined by its effect on behavior. Something that might be appealing to one person can serve as a punisher for another. A common example of this is publicly praising a teenager for something she has done. Although many younger children revel in public praise, this type of praise may embarrass a teenager rather than make her feel proud. This may, in turn, decrease the future probability of the teenager repeating the praised behavior.

Just as with reinforcement, there are positive and negative punishment procedures. In a **positive punishment** procedure, something is added to the environment (e.g., a lukewarm "fine" or praise) that weakens a behavior. With a **negative punishment** procedure, something is removed from the environment, leading to a decrease in a behavior. For example, removing privileges from a group home resident as a consequence for breaking a house rule might result in less rule-breaking in the future.

By definition, punishment leads to weakening, or unlearning, a response. If you think something is a punishment, but it doesn't change the behavior of the person you are trying to punish, then it is not a punishment to them. For example, if you "ground" your teenager for staying out too late, but the next time she goes out, she stays out late again, then being grounded is not really a punishment.

Including a punishment component in a behavior plan tends to enhance its effectiveness (Lerman & Vondran, 2002). For example, researchers have found that FBA-based plans that simply teach an appropriate alternative communication method are not as effective as those that add a punishment component to this intervention (Hanley, Piazza, Fisher & Maglieri, 2005). Nevertheless, there are numerous educational and ethical considerations in determining whether or not to incorporate a punishment component into a behavior plan, and in selecting an appropriate punishment. Guidelines for navigating this decision-making process are included in Chapter 5.

Keep It Simple Summary

1. A **reinforcer** strengthens (increases) behavior.
2. A **punisher** weakens (decreases) behavior.
3. The term **"positive"** means that something is added to the environment.
4. The term **"negative"** means that something is removed from the environment.

Consequence-Based Procedures

	Reinforcer	Punisher
Positive	Adding something strengthens behavior	Adding something weakens behavior
Negative	Taking away something strengthens behavior	Taking away something weakens behavior

Putting the Four Unlearning Variables Together

In order for learning to occur, all four variables—motivation, antecedent, behavior, and consequence—must be in place. Therefore, unlearning can occur by disrupting any of the variables, and is more likely to occur the more variables that are disrupted. For example, consider the example of Amos, above, who is hitting people in order to gain access to items he wants. Here are examples of how disrupting each of the four variables might lead to him unlearning his aggressive behavior:

1. Disrupting Motivation: If the MO for the objects is absent, then Amos will not hit his teacher. This might occur if Amos has just played with his favorite things.
2. Disrupting the Antecedent: If Amos's father is the only one who lets Amos have the items after hitting, and Amos's father is not there, Amos will not hit even if he is motivated to get the objects.
3. Disrupting the Behavior: Even if Amos is motivated to get the objects, and his father is present, Amos will not hit if his father is now providing the objects following a different behavior.
4. Disrupting the Consequence: Even if there is an MO for the objects and Amos's father is there, Amos will not hit if he is not given access to the items in response to hitting.

See Chapters 3–5 for detailed information about strategies to use in disrupting each of these variables.

3 | Beating the Behavior to the Punch:
Using Antecedent Strategies to Decrease a Behavior

You may have noticed in the previous chapter that a big part of the learning process happens even before the problem behavior occurs. Behavior intervention plans that are based on this first half of the learning process are called antecedent strategies. These strategies rely on altering:

1. the *motivative variables* that influence the person's motivation to engage in the problem behavior;

2. the *setting events* that make the behaviors more likely to occur in the face of weaker MO's (when the person's motivation is lower); and

3. the *discriminative variables* (S^D's, S^P's and $S^\triangle$'s) that cue the person whether or not the problem behavior is likely to get him what he wants under a specific set of circumstances.

Advantages of Using Antecedent Strategies

When selecting a behavior intervention strategy, antecedent strategies have a special appeal. One reason: when you use antecedent strategies, you are not in the position of responding to a problem behavior that has already wreaked havoc. Rather, antecedent strategies are put into place with the goal of preventing a behavior from occurring in the first place. This type of strategy is more peaceful and pleasant for the individual himself, as well as the people around him. By using your functional assessment data, you can introduce specific changes into the individual's environment that will improve his quality of life. This, in turn, makes it less likely that the person will need to use the problem behavior as a means of communication. These principles are at the heart of Positive Behavior Support (Carr, Horner, et al., 1999), which aims to use what we learn from challenging behaviors to better an individual's world.

Preventing the unwanted behavior has several advantages. First of all, if the person does not engage in the challenging behavior, then there are no negative effects, such as destruction or injury. While the antecedents are in place, the destructive behavior never happens, so no damage is done. An additional benefit of using antecedent strategies is that the individual is not practicing the problematic response. As we know from our knowledge of the learning process, the more someone practices a particular response, the more likely it is to be reinforced. This makes future occurrences of the problem behavior more likely. Antecedent interventions sidestep this risk.

The Disadvantage of Using Antecedent Strategies

There is also one significant disadvantage to using antecedent strategies. Because these interventions work by removing the motivation or cues for the person to engage in the problem behavior, he does not learn how to better respond in situations in which the motivation or cues are, in fact, present.

For example, consider Brandon, a student with autism who makes wisecracks in class. Let's imagine that an FBA has demonstrated that this behavior functions to obtain teacher attention, and that Brandon can go for about 15 minutes without being called on before he will make a wisecrack. Let's further imagine that Brandon can discriminate between teachers who ignore the wisecracks and teachers who scold him in response to wisecracks. An antecedent strategy targeting the MO might involve having teachers pay attention to Brandon's on-task behaviors every 10 minutes. This intervention would surely prevent the wisecracks, but would not teach Brandon what to do when he inevitably does want attention.

While this type of antecedent strategy may be a necessary step for the short term (e.g., to decrease class disruptions and minimize stigmatization of the student with autism), it may not be a sufficient intervention for the long-term. The teaching team has a responsibility to eventually teach this student how to get his need for attention met.

There are some situations where it is appropriate to keep an antecedent strategy in place indefinitely. For example, consider the all too-familiar case of an adult with autism in a group home who engages in destructive behavior in order to escape from boring, repetitive tasks. A permanent intervention based on enriching this individual's environment with stimulating and productive tasks is an ethical, reasonable, and appropriate choice.

Altering MOs and AOs

In order to create a behavior intervention plan based on altering Motivating Operations (MOs) and Abolishing Operations (AOs), you will need to know the MO for the challenging behavior. That is, what is going on in the environment that makes the person value a particular item or activity and exert himself to obtain it? You will also need to know the individual's MO threshold for launching into the problem behavior. That is, how long can he tolerate doing without the desired item or activity? You will then choose a strategy for preventing the MO from reaching that level.

The steps below are intended to guide you through the general process of altering MOs and AOs. Underneath each step's instruction is an example written in italics.

Step 1

The first step is to **identify the MO for your child's or student's response.** Be specific. You will be able to figure this out using your FBA results. For example:

> *Grace physically attacks peers in response to an MO*
> *for peer attention.*

Step 2

The second step is to *identify the threshold for the MO.* You may need to complete additional observations to gather this information. For example, you might:

- Time the *latency* until the problem response. The latency is the amount of time that passes after the start of an activity before the behavior occurs. For instance: For a student who has challenging behaviors during a group lesson, record the amount of time from the beginning of the group lesson until the onset of the problem behavior. This is the latency until the behavior. It tells us how long the student can tolerate whatever it is about group work that sets off the behavior.

- Count the number of demands that precede the problem behavior. For example, for a student who tends to engage in the problem behavior during class work, count how many instructions he can complete before he launches into the problem behavior. This tells us how much of the task the student can tolerate.

- Count the number of failed attempts the individual makes to complete a task before the problem response occurs. For example, some individuals engage in problem behaviors during challenging tasks. Count how many errors or failed attempts at something occur prior to the onset of the problem behavior. This tells us how much task-related frustration the individual can tolerate. For example:

  Grace attempts an average of 5 un-reinforced peer initiations before attacking the peer.

Step 3

Next, *choose an intervention strategy* from the following menu to alter the MO:

A. Calculate 75 percent of the individual's threshold—whether that threshold is measured in latency, number of demands, or failed attempts before the problem behavior occurs. Then provide the individual with the reinforcer he is seeking at that 75 percent level to prevent him from reaching his threshold for the problem response. If 75 percent falls between two numbers, provide the reinforcer at the lower number (i.e., shorter latency, fewer attempts). For example:

> *Grace's peers will be prompted to respond to her after Grace has made 3 initiations. (75 percent of her threshold of 5 attempts falls between 3 and 4, so 3 was chosen.)*

B. Provide the reinforcer on a noncontingent schedule. That is, regularly give the person his desired reinforcement, whether or not he is engaging in the problem behavior.

> *Every 5 minutes, provide a structured peer interaction for Grace.*

C. Present a competing MO. In other words, find something else the individual might want as much or more than the motivator leading to the problematic behavior. Identify some activities and objects that the person finds rewarding. Make one or more of them available as an alternative reinforcer at times the individual is likely to engage in the problem behavior.

> *When Grace will be around peers who are likely to be nonresponsive, offer her a favorite snack in another room.*

Step 4

The fourth step is to *collect baseline data.* A baseline is a measure of the behavior before any intervention begins. It paints a picture of what would happen with the behavior if no intervention were put in place. Baseline data are characterized by:

- level (is the behavior occurring often or intensively enough to warrant intervention?);
- trend (is it increasing or decreasing?); and
- variability (does it change every day or occur consistently?)

More information on baseline data is included in Chapter 8. Based on what makes the most sense with the type of behavior you are concerned about, select an appropriate unit of measure (frequency, latency, intensity, etc.).

    A. Observe and measure the behavior. Be sure all team members understand the measurement system.

    B. Continue observing and measuring the behavior in this fashion until a stable level and trend can be determined.

Step 5

The final step is to *implement the strategy.* Continue to take the same type of data collected at baseline. This may be implemented as part of a package, or one step at a time. Use phase change lines on the graph to indicate where you make the shift from baseline to intervention. If the intervention includes multiple steps, place a phase change line on the graph as each step is added to the plan. In other words, each change in the intervention should be represented by a different phase on the graph. (See Figure 3.)

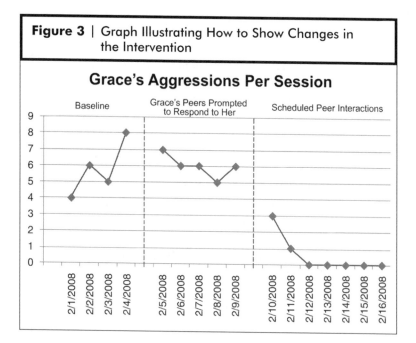

Figure 3 | Graph Illustrating How to Show Changes in the Intervention

Altering Discriminative Variables

Besides changing the factors that motivate someone to engage in a challenging behavior, you can also change the conditions that make it more likely that he will use the behavior. That is, you can create a behavior intervention plan based on altering discriminative variables. You can change either: 1) the discriminative stimuli (S^D's) which prompt him to do the behavior, or 2) the punishing stimuli (S^P's) that discourage him from doing the behavior.

To make this kind of behavior intervention plan, you will need to know the S^D's and S^P's for the challenging behavior. The general strategies you will incorporate will be either removing the S^D's or changing their meaning. The steps below are intended to guide you through the general process of altering S^D's. Again, underneath each step's instruction, an example is written in italics.

Step 1: Use information gathered through your FBA to identify S^D's and S^P's for the problem behavior. Consider under what conditions the behavior always occurs, and under what conditions the behavior never occurs. Are certain people present? Are certain objects present? Does the behavior occur when there are more or fewer people present? Does it occur during certain tasks? Does it occur only in public or private? For example:

> *Grace will bite any children who are similar in size to her or smaller. The presence of these children acts as an S^D.*

Step 2: Choose an intervention strategy from the following menu to alter the S^D's.
1. Eliminate the S^D's. If the person is not exposed to the cue that he can receive reinforcement for a certain behavior, he will not engage in the behavior.

> *Grace will be taught in a one-to-one setting until her biting is brought under control by other methods. (Alternatively, if feasible, Grace could be placed in a classroom with older, bigger children for certain subjects to continue to allow her to have group experiences.)*

2. Change the meaning of the S^D's by unlinking the stimulus from the outcome the person has been receiving for his challenging behavior. This can be accomplished by: a) changing the outcome the person receives for the challenging behavior, while keeping the original stimulus the same, and/or b) presenting the person with his desired outcome when he uses a different (more appropriate response) to the original stimulus.

> *Grace's classmates will be instructed to a) ignore Grace if she is aggressive, rather than yelling at her or trying to get her back, and b) provide an enthusiastic response to Grace's appropriate initiations.*

Step 3: Implement the strategy. Continue to gather the same type of data collected at baseline. This may be implemented as part of a package, or one step at a time. Use phase change lines on the graph to indicate the shift from baseline to intervention, and the addition of each component of intervention, as illustrated in Figure 3.

Addressing Important Setting Events

As discussed in Chapter 2, some challenging behaviors are influenced by events ("setting events") that take place a long time before the behavior occurs. The event that makes the problem behavior more likely might even take place when the person with autism is in a different setting or with different people than when he engages in the problem behavior.

The setting event may be something that occurs outside of the individual. For example, an adult with autism in a group home may have a roommate who sometimes makes loud, repetitive groans early in the morning, or a school-aged child with Asperger's disorder may hear his parents fighting in the morning. Alternately, the setting event may be something internal to the individual, such as an allergy attack or lack of sleep. Minimizing the likelihood that a setting event will lead to a problem behavior is often an important part of a behavior plan.

Step 1: Identify the setting events affecting the challenging behavior. You may have gotten this information from your FBA results. Otherwise, you may need to conduct further evaluation. The Setting

Events Menu in Appendix A may help with this process. Have each caregiver responsible for your child or student with autism fill it out for the duration of an FBA, or until a pattern is established during the behavior plan development process. Indicate on your behavior graph whether or not the setting event occurred within 24 hours of the challenging behavior (see Figure 4).

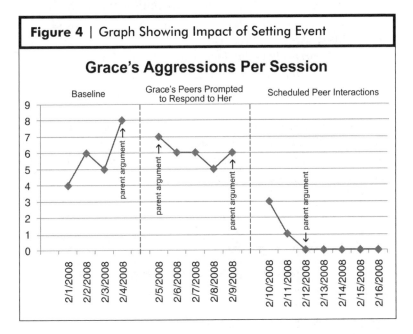

Figure 4 | Graph Showing Impact of Setting Event

If a setting event is identified, continue to fill out the checklist as a means of letting other caregivers know that the setting event is in effect. For example, if a child tends to have more flopping episodes when he has slept poorly the night before, his teachers will be alerted to nights of poor sleep when the student arrives in the morning with his checklist. This gives the teacher an opportunity to prevent related challenging behaviors by providing less physically demanding activities, or activities that generally require less effort.

Example of a setting event for Grace:

> *Grace is likely to physically attack peers after only two un-reinforced initiations if she has witnessed her parents having a fight in the morning.*

Step 2: Choose an intervention strategy from the following menu to ameliorate the effects of a setting event.

    A. Avoid the setting event.

       Instruct Grace's parents not to fight in front of her.

    B. Adjust demands on the person if you know the setting event has occurred. You must continue to complete the setting events checklist and share information with teachers, parents, and others to ensure effective use of this strategy.

       If parents have fought in Grace's presence, help Grace initiate appropriate interactions with her classmates and prompt them to respond to her.

Step 3: Implement the strategy. Continue to take the same type of data collected at baseline. Use phase change lines on the graph to indicate the shift from baseline to intervention, and the addition of each component of intervention, as shown in Figure 3.

Keep It Simple Summary

1. Antecedent interventions prevent the challenging behavior from occurring in the first place.
2. To use this approach, consider...
   - altering the motivation for the behavior,
   - altering the cues to engage in the behavior, and
   - responding to events that make the behavior more likely to occur.

4 | What Can He Do Instead? Building Replacement Skills for Problem Behaviors

In our review of the unlearning process, we saw that an essential component of eliminating one behavior is to teach the individual another behavior to take its place. At the heart of the FBA process is the understanding that problem behaviors are happening for a reason. They are communicating to us about something the individual needs. Once we understand what the problem behavior is communicating, we must teach replacement skills that leave the individual empowered with a better way to get the job done. But, how can we ensure that the individual will use the replacement behavior that we have chosen to get her needs met, rather than some other, less desirable behavior?

Factors That Affect Whether a Replacement Behavior Is Used

This section will discuss some general considerations to keep in mind when selecting a replacement behavior, and explain how to choose a skill that your child or student will actually use. Later in the book, Chapter 6 will go into specifics about matching a replacement behavior to the problem behavior's function.

How Frequently the Behavior Is Reinforced

In an effort to discover how living things choose among multiple means to the same end, psychologist Richard Herrnstein (1970) performed research on animals. This research demonstrated that how often an animal selects a specific response depends on the rate of reinforcement from that response. Since then, similar studies have been done with humans (e.g., Romanowich, Bourret, & Vollmer, 2007) and we know that people, too, are more likely to do the things that bring them the most rewards.

You have probably seen this play out in your everyday experiences. For example, imagine that your child has learned through experience that Mom and Dad are very unlikely to give her candy in response to whining, but are very likely to give her candy for completing her chores. If so, whenever she wants candy, then the rate of whining for candy will drop, while the rate of completing chores will rise. Completing chores is on a richer reinforcement schedule (i.e., rewarded better) than whining, and therefore replaces it.

How Quickly the Behavior Is Reinforced

Another aspect of reinforcement that influences whether an individual will choose to use a replacement behavior is the amount of time that passes between engaging in the behavior and receiving a rewarding response. All else being equal, the more immediately the person receives reinforcement for a behavior, the more likely she is to select it.

Consider, for example, choosing between two jobs that offer the same salary and have the same demands. Imagine that one job pays you every other week, and the other job pays you one year after you start it. Almost everyone would choose the more immediate payment. This helps to explain why many students with autism engage in challenging behavior. It is not uncommon for the "squeaky wheel" to get the grease. In other words, the child who makes an appropriate request is often asked to wait a few minutes for her requested item. In contrast, a student who screams a request and disrupts the class may be more likely to get an immediate response. The latter child is choosing the more immediate paycheck.

When selecting replacement skills for problem behaviors, we must choose skills that are likely to get immediate reinforcement for the student and arrange the environment to ensure that this occurs. For example, the screaming student mentioned above must be taught not only how to make an appropriate request (she may already know this) but also that her appropriate response will be reinforced more immediately than her screaming. Remember, the individual is engaging in the problem behavior because it is the most efficient way to get what she wants. An analogy may help to clarify this point: If I want my husband's attention during the March Madness basketball tournament, I certainly could say, "Excuse me," and begin speaking, but I may not get his immediate or full attention. Alternatively, I could stand in front of the television or turn it off and he would immediately begin speaking to me. Although the quality of what he says may be less than polite, if I am motivated purely by attention, the quality of that attention may not be critical to me. Instead, any intense attention may reinforce my "problem" response.

When working with students, we can use this principle of immediacy to encourage the behaviors that we'd like to see more of and discourage the behaviors that we'd like to see disappear. For example, if a student is calling out in class because she wants the teacher's attention, the teacher might call on the student immediately when she raises her hand. Over time, as the student becomes very likely to raise her hand and very unlikely to call out, we can begin teaching the student to wait for attention. Similarly, if a student is destroying furniture to escape work, we can teach that student that she can have a break upon request. Again, other interventions can address the student's motivation to request a break, as well as her ability to wait for a break. In the meantime, furniture destruction is prevented, and appropriate break requests are strengthened.

Not every request can be reinforced immediately. For example, if your child wants a particular type of ice cream dessert only available from *Friendly's,* and the closest *Friendly's* is 45 miles away, you obviously cannot reinforce her request immediately. However, in this situation, the dessert will not be provided immediately even if your child "requests" it with the problem behavior. Therefore, the immediacy of reinforcement was not responsible for your child originally learning the problem behavior and therefore does not need to be part of the intervention plan.

Over time, the delay between the replacement behavior and reinforcement can be systematically increased to a typical length of time. But this should only occur when the student is reliably using the replacement behavior and when other aspects of intervention (cues when immediate reinforcement is available, scheduled access to desired item, and a waiting skills program) are in place.

How Much and How Well the Behavior Is Reinforced

The magnitude and quality of a reinforcer also affect which behaviors a person will choose to engage in. All else being equal, if a greater amount of reinforcement or better quality reinforcement is available for one response as compared to another, then the person will select that response. For example, Hannah Hoch and her colleagues (2002) demonstrated that children with autism who typically preferred to play alone could be taught to choose to play with peers or siblings if this resulted in opportunities to play with better toys for longer periods of time.

When choosing replacement behaviors for someone, we must choose responses likely to lead to reinforcement that rivals the reinforcement received for the problem behavior in magnitude and quality. For example, if the problem behavior leads to an animated, high-intensity reprimand, then the attention paid to the replacement behavior must be animated and high intensity. A simple, "Good job," will not do the trick. Instead, an intense, "Woohoo! Awesome!" paired with a high five and a little dance might be more effective. Likewise, if hitting a classmate allows a student to escape from the demands of the classroom and visit the principal's office for an hour, responding to the student's appropriate break request with a five-minute break will not be effective. Instead, the reinforcer for the appropriate behavior must rival that for the challenging behavior.

How Much Effort Is Required to Perform the Behavior

A final variable to consider when selecting a replacement behavior is the balance between the effort required to perform the behavior and the reinforcement the individual receives for doing it. Researcher R. Don Tustin (1994) described this as "behavioral economics." In short, individuals will pay a different "price," in terms of effort, for different "products." All else being equal, people select the behavior that requires the least amount of effort. Therefore, the less effort a replacement skill requires, the more likely the individual is to use it instead of the problem behavior.

Typically, people with autism are pretty good at their problem behaviors. These behaviors are unfortunately well-practiced and self-selected for simplicity. In short, they require little effort, and are, therefore, tough to compete with.

With planning, however, low-effort alternatives to problem behaviors can be identified. For example, for problem behaviors related to escaping demands, a low-effort alternative that often works is to put a large break card on the student's desk and teach her to tap it to request a break. Or, for an adult with autism who uses inappropriate behavior to request items, an intervention as simple as having her wear her augmentative communication system on a strap, so she does not have to get up and get it, may result in her using the system to make requests.

Using *precision teaching* to build fluency is always recommended when teaching replacement skills (West, Young, & Spooner, 1990). Precision teaching focuses on building speed, as well as accuracy, in performing a skill, and in doing so systematically with gradually increasing demands on the student to ensure continued success. The more fluent a response is for an individual, the less effort it requires. From a prevention perspective, it's best to teach all skills to fluency to ensure that your child or student has a sufficient repertoire of simple, appropriate responses to prevent the development of inappropriate compensatory responses.

Choosing a Reinforcement-Based Strategy

As you can see from the above variables influencing an individual's choice of response, it is impossible to completely separate out each component of the learning equation when looking at problem behaviors. Reinforcement in particular is closely linked to the behaviors that people with autism spectrum disorders choose to engage in.

There are three reinforcement-based strategies that can be used to help your child or student substitute a replacement skill for a problem behavior:

1. Differential Reinforcement of Alternative behaviors (DRA),
2. Differential Reinforcement of Incompatible behaviors (DRI), and

3. Differential Reinforcement of High Rates of Behavior (DRH).

All of these strategies rely on "differential" reinforcement, meaning that the problem behavior and the appropriate behavior each receive different levels of reinforcement. To strengthen the replacement skill, you ensure that it leads to more reinforcement than the problem behavior does. Note that if you use these strategies, you do not have to make a formal plan for extinction of the problem behavior. You may choose not to reinforce the problem behavior at all, or you may choose to reinforce it just a little to prevent an extinction burst (as discussed in Chapter 5). As long as the replacement skill leads to greater reinforcement for the individual than the problem behavior does, it will still replace it.

Differential Reinforcement of Alternative Behaviors (DRA)

To use DRA, you differentially reinforce another, more appropriate means of communicating the same message as the problem behavior. Specifically, you arrange for the individual to get a great deal of reinforcement for using the replacement behavior and little (or no) reinforcement for using the problem behavior.

Consider the case of Jamaal, whose problem behavior (using odd postures when other children come near him) communicates that he'd like to escape interacting with peers. A DRA for Jamaal might entail teaching him that he can end any interaction by saying, "See you later," and walking away. Jamaal will first be prompted to practice this skill when it is believed that a relevant MO is in effect (that is, when he is motivated to escape from an interaction). Prompts will gradually be faded until Jamaal can independently exit the interaction.

Differential reinforcement begins even while the substitute response is still being prompted to make sure that the individual learns the new behavior. At the same time, teachers will ensure that Jamaal's posturing and odd faces will not succeed in getting him out of interactions with peers. They might establish a consequence for the problem behavior in which Jamaal is prompted to make two more comments before being allowed to walk away from the other child. Providing differential reinforcement for the replacement behavior (allowing

Jamaal to leave the interaction immediately) will lead to the cessation of the problem behavior.

Jamaal's example also highlights the important role an FBA plays in identifying needed changes to the curriculum, as well as the need for multi-pronged intervention. For the long term, it is not sufficient that Jamaal escape every interaction, even appropriately. Jamaal also needs to improve his social skills so that he can interact more appropriately with other children. Therefore, while this plan is in effect, other interventions that will make peer interactions more appealing to Jamaal should also be put in place. For example, providing Jamaal with better quality reinforcement when he spends time with peers, as was the case with the study mentioned above (Hoch et al., 2002), might be a separate component of the plan.

Differential Reinforcement of Incompatible Behaviors (DRI)

Like a DRA, a DRI identifies a replacement behavior that will lead to the person receiving a greater degree and quality of the reinforcer than she has been receiving in response to her problem behavior. However, a DRI involves teaching the individual a replacement behavior that is *incompatible* with the problem behavior. Specifically, it will not be possible to perform the problem behavior and the incompatible behavior at the same time.

For example, recall Grace, and her habit of attacking other students to get their attention. If she is paired with a buddy to play hand games (e.g., "Miss Mary Mac," or "Oh, Little Playmate"), she cannot hit the other child and play these games at the same time. In addition, the nature of the game ensures that she will receive a high level of peer attention for using the replacement behavior. Similarly, if a boy has learned to flap his hands because it has led to the OT providing deep pressure in the form of a back massage, he can be given a back massage while he completes his written assignments (which requires the appropriate use of his hands and cannot be completed while flapping). Or, if a child has been reinforced for screaming her requests for ice cream, then she can be taught that only quiet requests for ice cream will actually lead to ice cream. She cannot possibly scream and use a quiet voice at the same time.

There will not be an appropriate incompatible behavior to reinforce for every challenging behavior, but if you think creatively, you will often come up with a way to use this relatively simple yet effective intervention.

Differential Reinforcement of High Rates of Behavior (DRH)

To use DRH, you gradually increase your demands on the individual to use an appropriate behavior in place of a problem behavior. Specifically, you require her to perform a particular behavior, at a systematically increasing rate, in order to receive the desired reinforcer.

The first step of a DRH is to calculate a baseline rate for use of the replacement skill. For example, if we want Thomas, a group home resident, to complete his job of folding the laundry rather than using self-injurious behavior to escape this task, we would first want to know how much laundry he will fold before injuring himself. Next, establish a system that allows Thomas to earn the reinforcer (a break from folding laundry) for achieving specific rates of folding. The first session's goal should be about 75 percent of the baseline rate. This increases the likelihood that any given individual will earn the reinforcer, which will strengthen the appropriate response (increase the likelihood that the person will do it again). In the example above, if Thomas will fold four articles of clothing before he begins injuring himself, then the task should be considered complete and removed (the reinforcer for the problem behavior), after he has folded only three articles of clothing. The goal should increase systematically. Continuing our example, we might increase the demands on Thomas by one additional article of clothing after each three consecutive days without self-injury.

Determining Whether to Use DRA, DRI, or DRH

Any of the above differential reinforcement interventions may be used for a given problem behavior. Unfortunately, there are no clear guidelines as to which one to select for a specific situation. Instead, the decision is made simply by thinking through which approach would make the most sense. Consider the following example:

Maddie is an eight-year-old girl with autism who continues to run into her parents' bedroom and jump into their bed in the middle of the night. Specifically, Maddie wants to sleep next to her mother. This is the reinforcer for running to her parents' room in the middle of the night. Which differential reinforcement strategy might encourage Maddie to stay in her own bed? To determine this, we must think through each strategy.

Could we use a DRA? This would involve identifying and strengthening an appropriate alternative response that would still lead to the reinforcer (sleeping next to Mom). Because sleeping with her mother is, in fact, a problem, there is no appropriate alternative. A DRA can be ruled out.

Can we use a DRI? To do so, we would need to strengthen a behavior that is incompatible with running to her parents' bed and that will still lead to the reinforcer (sleeping next to Mom). The only possible behavior that might fit that criterion is teaching Maddie to call for her mother from her bed, and then her mother could go sleep in Maddie's bed with her. This is probably no better for the family than having Maddie run into her parents' bedroom, and may be even worse, as it requires Mom to wake up more fully and sleep less comfortably. A DRI can be ruled out.

Next, think through a DRH. To use this strategy, Maddie would have to practice a more desirable behavior (i.e., staying in bed) at gradually increasing rates. This might be accomplished by having the mother go to get Maddie at a certain time and bring her into bed (which breaks the contingency between Maddie running into her parents' room and getting access to Mom, and builds a connection between staying in bed and getting access to Mom). The time that Mom goes to get Maddie could then be systematically pushed back. If Maddie

Keep It Simple Summary

- One behavior will replace another only if it is reinforced at least as often as the problem behavior is reinforced.
- A replacement behavior must also compete with the problem behavior in terms of immediacy, magnitude, and quality of the reinforcer.
- A replacement behavior must require less effort than the problem behavior.
- Types of differential reinforcement strategies are:
    - ❑ DRA—differential reinforcement of alternative behavior,
    - ❑ DRI—differential reinforcement of incompatible behavior, and
    - ❑ DRH—differential reinforcement of high rates of behavior.

runs into her parents' room before that time, she will be brought back to her own bed. In this way, Maddie could be taught to sleep through the whole night, and cuddle with Mom in the morning. The DRH is therefore a feasible intervention.

As demonstrated above, there is no rule that specifies which strategy to use. Instead, you will have to carefully consider your options and make a reasonable choice.

5 | Consequence-based Strategies

You may have noticed in our discussion of the first three components of the learning equation that each of the earlier components was influenced to some degree by consequences for behavior. Changing consequences is the most pivotal approach to changing behavior, and for most interventions is a necessary component.

There are two broad strategies for changing behavior:
1. reinforcement-based strategies, and
2. punishment-based strategies.

These consequences are at the heart of all behavior change, as their sole function is to increase or decrease behavior, respectively.

Reinforcement

A "reinforcer" is a consequence that strengthens a behavior. In other words, reinforcement is something that immediately follows a behavior that increases the probability of that behavior occurring in similar situations in the future.

You can't tell a reinforcer by looking at it. You can only tell a reinforcer by its effect on an individual's behavior. Something that looks very appealing to one person may not be at all appealing to another. Furthermore, the ability of a consequence to act as a reinforcer varies with Motivating Operations (MOs). For example, if you like pizza, one slice of pizza at lunchtime is likely to act as a reinforcer for any behavior you might use to obtain the pizza (e.g., going to the pizza place, ordering pizza, and paying for it). Once you have had your fill of pizza, though, a fourth or fifth slice of pizza might even act as a punisher for you.

As explained in Chapter 2, problem behaviors, like all behaviors, are learned through their relationship to reinforcement. That is, a person will learn to engage in a problem behavior if he regularly receives reinforcement for doing that behavior. A functional behavior assessment identifies the reinforcers that strengthen a given problem behavior. The strategies below highlight how to use the reinforcers identified for your child or student in careful ways to help him unlearn the problem behavior.

In the previous chapter, three differential reinforcement strategies were discussed: DRA, DRI, and DRH. Those strategies aimed to reduce a problem behavior by increasing some other specific behaviors. Two additional differential reinforcement strategies will be described below. Although the strategies described in this chapter are also referred to as "differential reinforcement," their names are misleading. In fact, they focus more on reducing the problem behavior than on strengthening an alternative behavior. The emphasis of these interventions is on providing the individual with desired items and activities to weaken the problem behavior.

Differential Reinforcement of Low Rates of Behavior (DRL)

In the previous chapter, differential reinforcement of high rates of behavior (DRH) was introduced as a strategy to encourage someone to use an appropriate replacement behavior more often than the problem behavior. DRL works along those same lines. But instead of reinforcing the individual for an increased rate of a replacement behavior, DRL reinforces the individual for a decreased rate of the problem behavior.

This is a good approach for gradually decreasing problem behaviors that are initially occurring quite often. While you might try to teach a replacement skill at the same time you are reducing the problem behavior, the DRL does not rely on teaching a replacement skill to reduce the behavior. An everyday example of using the DRL approach might be a smoker who decides to quit by setting up a system that allows him to smoke one fewer cigarette per day until he has quit. Perhaps this smoker might also get a dollar in a "luxuries fund" for each day that he smokes the designated number of cigarettes or fewer.

An example of using this approach with a child with autism may be seen in the case of Marie. Marie's problem behavior was swearing. At baseline, she swore an average of 125 times per day. An FBA revealed that Marie's swearing functioned to get attention from a favorite teacher. A DRL was implemented in which she was allowed five fewer swear words per day in order to obtain her reinforcer: 15 minutes of special time with her favorite teacher. To increase Marie's chances of success, once she was only swearing 20 times per day, the allowed "swears" were reduced by only one each day.

From the beginning, Marie's teachers used a token board to help her visualize how many "swears" she had left. The teachers made a chart with 125 Velcro circles on it, and at first 125 pictures of the favorite teacher were on the board. One little picture was removed each time Marie swore. If there were any pictures left at the end of the day, Marie was allowed to spend 15 minutes with her preferred teacher. When the number of swears allowed was reduced, the day began with fewer pictures of the teacher on the chart. After approximately two months of the intervention, Marie was down to zero swearing incidents per day, and one year later, her problem behavior had not recurred.

Keep It Simple Summary

To implement a DRL:
1. Calculate the baseline rate of the problem behavior.
2. Set a schedule for gradually reducing the behavior. As a guide, do not reduce the rate by more than 25 percent per day. More gradual rates of reduction are acceptable and should vary depending on the student. It is more important for your child or student to succeed in obtaining the reinforcer each day than to reduce the behavior quickly.
3. Provide your child or student with the reinforcer identified in the FBA if he keeps his behavior at the designated level for the agreed-upon period of time.
4. If the rate of problem behaviors exceeds the criteria, do not provide reinforcement.
5. If your child or student continues to exceed the designated level for the problem behavior for three consecutive days/sessions, reconvene the intervention team for troubleshooting.

Differential Reinforcement of Other Behaviors (DRO)

The term DRO is widely used, and is actually a misnomer. In a DRO procedure, no specific "other" behavior is actually strengthened. Instead, a DRO involves providing the person with reinforcement whenever he does not perform the problem behavior for a given period of time. Initially, the person is reinforced after a very small interval of time, to ensure that he succeeds in obtaining the reinforcer. The interval is then systematically increased. A DRO is sometimes referred to as Differential Reinforcement of Zero Rates of Responding, or DRZ. This describes the procedure more accurately.

Although the DRO intervention is commonly used to reduce problem behaviors, you should keep the following cautions in mind when deciding whether to use it:

The Need to Identify and Teach a Replacement Behavior

Despite the name, no replacement behavior is actually taught with a DRO. Be sure to use another procedure to strengthen an alternative behavior or your child or student will not learn what to do instead of the problem behavior.

For example, if an FBA determines that Joey is repetitively screaming, "Cheez-It!" as a means of obtaining Cheez-It crackers, a DRO might involve him earning a Cheez-It for every five minutes that he goes without screaming for a cracker. There is no specific alternative behavior that we want him to do to obtain a Cheez-It. He simply must not scream, "Cheez-It!" Even if Joey screams something else, asks politely for a Cheez-It, or engages in a different problem behavior, at the end of the five-minute interval, he would earn his Cheez-It. However, he is not being taught how to appropriately request a Cheez-It, should he want one.

Nevertheless, a DRO can be used in conjunction with a DRA. For example, Joey could be offered a Cheez-It noncontingently at the end of every five minute interval without screaming, and also receive one in response to an appropriate request.

The Need to Identify and Use a Variety of Reinforcers

When used as an intervention for a problem behavior that occurs very frequently, the initial interval for a DRO might be very short. I have seen DROs as short as 10 seconds for behaviors that occurred so often that the child or student otherwise would have been unlikely to receive reinforcement.

When an individual is reinforced so frequently, the risk of becoming satiated (getting too much of the reinforcer) is high. To prevent satiation

---

Keep It Simple Summary

To implement a DRO:

1. Calculate the average latency (amount of time) from the end of one instance of the problem behavior to the beginning of the next.
2. Set the initial interval for providing reinforcement at 75 percent of the average latency.
3. Set a criterion for increasing the interval. A common criterion might be to increase the interval once the person is successful during 90 percent of the intervals per day across three consecutive days. Do not increase the interval by more than 25 percent at a time.
4. Identify a reinforcer or a pool of reinforcers that can be provided to the individual for successfully refraining from the behavior for the designated interval.
5. Select a fixed or variable DRO. A DRO may be at a fixed interval (the same interval every time) or a variable interval (different intervals every time that average out to the target interval). In busy settings, choose a fixed interval to make it easier to implement the DRO, and a variable interval when possible to prevent your child or student from looking for reinforcement at a certain time. To use a variable interval, it is easiest to create a list of times that will average to a certain interval and write them out in random order before working with the individual. Cross off each interval from the list as it is completed. For example, a one-minute variable interval might include the following intervals: 30 seconds, 90 seconds, 1 minute, immediate, 2 minutes. Use a digital timer to simplify this process.
6. Select an interval DRO or momentary DRO. An interval DRO is used when you will observe your child or student throughout the whole interval and reinforce him only if he refrains from the behavior for the whole interval. A momentary DRO is used either for very high rates of behavior, or for situations when the individual cannot be observed for the entire interval. It involves providing the reinforcer if the problem behavior is absent at the moment the interval ends.
7. If the criterion for increasing the interval is not met for three consecutive days/sessions, reconvene the intervention team for troubleshooting.

when using DROs with short intervals, consider offering various preferred items rather than relying only on the reinforcer identified in the FBA. Keep in mind, however, that identifying what will act as a reinforcer at a given moment can be tricky and will be essential to the success of the DRO. For more guidance on choosing reinforcers, you may want to read *Incentives for Change: Motivating People with Autism Spectrum Disorders to Learn and Gain Independence* (L. Delmolino and S. Harris, 2004).

Extinction

In contrast to differential reinforcement procedures, extinction involves stopping reinforcement for a problem behavior altogether. With extinction, reinforcement levels for one behavior are not compared to reinforcement levels for competing behaviors. Instead, extinction focuses only on the problem behavior and ensures that no reinforcement is provided for it. For example, if your child typically gets you to buy him treats in the grocery store by screaming loudly for candy, ignoring his screams (if you can!) will ultimately lead to the demise of the screaming.

DRLs and DROs, along with DRHs, DRAs, and DRIs, may or may not include extinction as a component. That is, they may or may not require that you stop reinforcing the problem behavior. Instead, they might involve providing low levels of reinforcement for the problem behavior and immediate, intense reinforcement for the replacement behavior. This would prevent an "extinction burst." (As discussed in Chapter 2, during an extinction burst, the behavior initially increases before it decreases.).

To continue our example, once you start ignoring your child's screams for candy, he may progress from screaming to throwing groceries or hitting his sister in an attempt to obtain candy before he finally quits. Eventually, however, the failure of his behaviors to produce candy will lead to the cessation of those behaviors.

Although extinction is an effective intervention for problem behaviors, it must be used cautiously because of the potential for an extinction burst. Never use extinction for behaviors that either begin with, or may escalate to, serious aggression, self-injury, or significant property destruction. Additionally, extinction may not be effective for low-frequency behaviors, since the individual will not have many opportunities to learn that the problem behavior is no longer leading to reinforcement. For example, if your child or student only engages in a behavior every other month, in six months he would only have the experience of engaging in the problem behavior and failing to get the reinforcer three times.

For extinction to work, you must be able to keep the problem behavior from leading to any reinforcement. Therefore, it is not a good choice if it is difficult to prevent a given behavior from being reinforced. This is usually the case with automatically reinforcing behaviors—for instance, if a student hits his head in order to experience the resulting sensation. It is hard to prevent the reinforcing sensation with these types of behaviors. Likewise, extinction is the wrong intervention if others in the environment will have difficulty refraining from reacting in a way that the individual finds rewarding. For example, if a student tells inappropriate jokes to get attention, but they are actually funny, people might have a hard time keeping a straight face.

Keep in mind that when used in isolation, extinction will not provide the individual with an alternative way to get his needs met. We always want to ensure that our students have some way to communicate effectively.

Keep It Simple Summary

To implement extinction:

1. Once an FBA has identified what the reinforcer is for your child's or student's problematic behavior, do not provide the reinforcer following the behavior any more.
2. Be sure that the reinforcer is not being provided another way. For example, if peers have been providing desired attention by trying to talk your student out of the problem behavior, make sure they do not switch to giving him another form of attention such as reprimanding him for the behavior.
3. If a behavior that occurs at least once a day does not decrease in rate, magnitude, or duration after two weeks of trying extinction, reconvene the behavior intervention team for troubleshooting.

Punishment

Chapter 2 defines punishment as a consequence that weakens a behavior. In other words, punishment immediately follows a behavior, and, as a result, decreases the probability of that behavior occurring in similar situations in the future. Like reinforcement, you can't tell punishment by looking at it. You can only identify a punisher by its effect on behavior.

As with reinforcement, the ability of a consequence to act as a punisher varies with an individual's Motivating Operations and Abolishing Operations. For example, consider a teenager who is expecting an uncomfortable confrontation with a peer after school. If that teenager snaps at his father and is grounded as a result, the conflict with his peer has been avoided. In the future, in a similar situation, that teenager is likely to snap at his father again. Due to a fleeting MO (a motivation for snapping at his father that is not usually there), the father's intended punishment (grounding the teenager) has inadvertently acted as a reinforcer.

In 2002, Dorothea Lerman and Kristina Vondran reviewed the existing literature on punishment and summarized a number of important aspects of punishment:

1. Punishment procedures are often effective in reducing problem behaviors.
2. Punishment is rarely used in isolation, without other reinforcement-based procedures.
3. Most clinical studies of punishment have studied negative punishment. In other words, researchers have mostly studied what happens when you take something away from somebody as punishment (such as taking away points or money), rather than what happens when you add something to the environment (such as yelling, spanking, or having the child write sentences such as "I will not spit" over and over) as a punishment. In their study, Lerman and Vondran raised a concern that the effects of positive punishment procedures may not be well predicted by the studies that have been typically conducted.

Punishment can also lead to unpredictable side effects. These effects have been described as "unconditioned emotional responses." For example, the person may respond with unexpected aggression or emotion, and he may start to avoid many conditions associated with the punisher rather than just the punisher itself. For example, if a student is frequently punished by a specific teacher in school, he may quickly learn to avoid school altogether. Because people with autism and related disorders already have social skill deficits, be very cautious in selecting or devising punishment procedures that may make your child or student even more reluctant to interact socially with others.

Despite these concerns, various studies argue in favor of including punishment as an option for behavior intervention plans. For example, one group of researchers (Hanley et al., 2005) found that some individuals with autism made better progress when behavioral intervention included both reinforcement for using an alternative form of communication and punishment than they did with just reinforcement for using the alternative communication. Surprisingly, these researchers also found that these same individuals actually preferred the treatment with the punishment component. In a separate study, participants also preferred having an intervention as compared with just being allowed to perform the problem behavior (Dozier et al., 2007). The intervention in the latter study did not include a punishment component, however. This suggests that punishment is not the key ingredient in designing an intervention that will be appealing to an individual with autism.

Positive vs. Negative Punishment

As mentioned above, there are two types of punishment: 1) positive punishment, and 2) negative punishment. In a positive punishment procedure, an aversive (something the individual finds unpleasant) is added to the environment as a consequence for a particular behavior. For example, a spanking would be considered a positive punisher, as would washing out a child's mouth with soap for saying a bad word. Less intrusive positive punishment procedures might include a stern reprimand, or changing a student's green card to yellow in a "traffic light" system in a classroom.

When using positive punishers, it is important to prevent the individual from developing a "tolerance" for a punisher. For example, sternly reprimanding your child might be effective in reducing his behavior at first, but he might develop a tolerance for your reprimands and increase his problem behavior again. In turn, this might encourage you to increase the reprimand to a yell. When your child's behavior ceases to be affected by yelling, your responses may continue to escalate. This may set up a dangerous escalation and risk for abuse.

In a negative punishment procedure, something that the individual desires is taken away as a consequence for a problem behavior.

Examples include loss of privileges, dessert, television time, a favorite toy, etc. As with reinforcement-based procedures, you need to analyze FBA results to identify an appropriate punisher. Again, try to avoid a cycle where you take away all of the individual's privileges one by one in a cycle of escalating contingencies.

When to Consider Using Punishment

In sum, there are a variety of concerns associated with using punishment procedures. Nevertheless, when used correctly, punishments are effective and benefit the individual with the problem behavior.

As a general rule, I recommend first trying to develop behavior plans without punishment components. If, for some reason, the problem behavior does not decrease as desired, I would consider adding a punisher. There are two exceptions when I would consider using a punishment procedure immediately: 1) for a dangerous behavior, or 2) for a behavior that otherwise needs to be addressed quickly (for example, if your daughter with autism yells out in church and her sister is getting married in a church in a few weeks).

Also, generally speaking, you should always try a negative punishment procedure prior to a positive punishment procedure. Consider positive punishment procedures (adding something punishing to the person's environment) only after every other possible strategy has proven ineffective, and you have double checked the function of the behavior and have documented appropriate treatment integrity (see the troubleshooting tips in Chapter 10).

Self-management

When using consequence-based interventions, you can provide the consequence to your child or student with autism, or you can teach him to give himself the consequence through "self-management" techniques. In self-management, the person learns to make a response that is designed to control the problem behavior. For example, if I put a star on the calendar each full day that I stay on my diet, I am using positive reinforcement for sticking to the diet. Conversely, if I put a dollar in a jar to give away each day that I break my diet, I am using a negative punishment procedure to try to decrease my over-eating. When the person who provides the reinforcement or punishment is the same person whose behavior will be changed, this is called "self-management."

People with varying abilities can be taught to use self-management procedures. Teaching individuals to manage their own behavior has numerous advantages. First of all, the behavior manager is always with the person whose behavior needs to be changed. This makes the behavior change more likely to generalize across settings. Second, if a precursor to a behavior problem cannot be seen externally (e.g., a thought or feeling), self-management can still occur. For example,

Keep It Simple Summary

To implement self-management:
1. Develop an intervention plan. Involve the individual in forming the plan, if possible.
2. Teach the individual to recognize the behavior you want him to either reinforce or punish by using prompting and reinforcement for recognizing the behavior. With the student described above, we simply had his classroom aide subtly signal him with a hand on his shoulder when he was speaking to himself. People usually easily learn to identify behaviors that will be reinforced. When you are teaching someone to recognize a behavior to punish, it is typically a good idea for the person to receive less of a punisher if he notices the behavior on his own than if he has to be prompted. For example, a student might lose one token if he recognizes the behavior on his own and two if he must be prompted.
3. Systematically fade prompting based on planned criteria (for example, reduce prompting after three consecutive successful days at a given prompt level). Continue to reinforce the student for recognizing the behavior.
4. Once the individual is recognizing the behavior independently, systematically fade prompts used to administer the reinforcement or punishment.
5. Periodically do spot checks of whether the individual is self-managing the behavior appropriately.
6. Allow the individual to manage the behavior independently.
7. Continue to evaluate data. As with any other plan, if three days pass without progress, reconvene the intervention team for troubleshooting.

self-management may be very useful for automatic reinforcement behaviors. Third, self-management requires fewer resources, as less staff time and attention are required. Finally, self-management is the ultimate goal of any behavior plan, since it offers independence.

Consider self-management for people who are working toward autonomy in other ways (e.g., they are participating in an inclusive classroom or in supervised employment). Also, consider self-management for people who have been successful for some time with their behavior plan and may be able to use self-management as a step toward fading out the intervention. Finally, consider self-management to help raise your child's or student's awareness of a problem behavior. For example, one student I worked with was talking to himself nearly constantly. He did not seem to notice that he was doing it, but it disturbed the other students in his inclusive classroom. Learning self-management techniques helped him to realize when he was speaking and when he was being quiet. Because he was motivated to be accepted by his peers and not disturb them, just becoming aware of his self-talk helped him to significantly reduce the amount of self-talk.

Ethical Considerations

The Behavior Analyst Certification Board has a number of ethical guidelines that will be particularly helpful for anyone using consequence-based procedures. Anyone who is involved in behavior change should read, understand, and adhere to these guidelines. These guidelines are briefly summarized below, but this short review is not a substitute for complete knowledge of the guidelines. The full guidelines are available on the website of the Behavioral Analyst Certification Board at www.bacb.com/consum_frame.html under "Guidelines for Responsible Conduct."

Obtain written informed consent, from the individual or his guardian, for any behavior change procedure. Consent must be given without any perceived coercion on the part of the client. In other words, the individual or his guardian must feel that accepting or rejecting the proposed behavior plan will not result in any loss of services or privileges (e.g., "We cannot keep him at the group home if you don't consent to this plan" or, "He won't be able to stay in this school if you don't agree to this plan"). The individual giving consent must understand the plan being presented, and must understand his right to terminate the program at any time. (See Chapter 9 for a sample consent form.)

1. The plan must be based on proven scientific procedures, have a reasonable likelihood of success, and be based on the results of an FBA.
2. Choose plans based on reinforcement rather than punishment whenever possible. If punishment procedures are necessary, be sure to include reinforcement for an alternative behavior.
3. Use the intervention that is the least likely to cause any hardship, unpleasantness, or limitations on the individual while still likely to be effective.
4. Continually measure the behavior to assess the plan's effectiveness. Adjust and/or terminate the plan as indicated by criteria in the plan. Obtain consent from the individual or his guardian for any modifications.

6 | Sensible Interventions for Every Function

You know the function of the problem behavior. You know the basic principles of unlearning behavior. You know the general strategies of behavior change. You now have all of the ingredients necessary to prepare a sensible behavior intervention plan for your child or student.

In this chapter, a step-by-step approach will be used to help you create this plan. A menu of suggestions for each strategy type (antecedent-based, replacement skill, consequence-based) is included for each function (escape, attention, access to items and activities, automatic reinforcement). For each problem behavior, you will need to use at least one of each type of strategy. Therefore, every plan will include antecedent strategies, replacement skills, and altered consequences. Not every idea will be a match for every behavior problem. However, there should be sufficient ideas to choose from for each behavior problem you may face. You may choose to modify an idea to meet the needs of a particular problem behavior.

The sections below outline ideas for each main function of problem behaviors. Later in this book, there is a discussion of strategies for combining the ideas presented here in order to address behaviors that serve more than one function.

Ideas for Addressing Behaviors Maintained by Escape or Avoidance

Step 1: Clarify Understanding of the Function of the Behavior

Be sure that you know:
- What is the person escaping/avoiding?
- Why is the person trying to escape/avoid this?
    - Is it too hard?
    - Does she lack prerequisite skills?
    - Is it too easy?
    - Is it too boring?
    - Is it too repetitive?
    - Is there an aversive sensation involved?
    - Does the person exhibit the problem behavior before the activity even starts? As it is starting? At the beginning of the activity? How long does the person engage in the behavior?

You will need the above information to alter the task in such a way that it will no longer create an MO for escape or avoidance. For example, if the person begins the problem behavior as soon as the demand is placed on her, the demand itself must be aversive to her and therefore the demand will need to be reevaluated. However, if the individual complies with the demand for a while before beginning the behavior, then we know we have to either shorten the demand or build up the individual's endurance. Once you know the answers to the above questions, you are ready to move on to Step 2.

Step 2: Antecedent Strategies

Choose one or more of the **antecedent strategies** below. An illustration of each strategy follows in italics.

A. **Alter the demand.** Consider:
- Incorporating preferred materials into the task (to pair the task with reinforcement). *Instead of teaching your child to count using squares or dots, have her count something she loves, such as dinosaurs.*

- Making the task more challenging (if the assessment reveals the demand is too simple). *Instead of simply counting, count group members, and add up groups.*
- Making the task less challenging (if the assessment reveals the demand is too challenging). *Instead of adding groups, simply count group members.*
- Building fluent prerequisite skills (if the assessment reveals the demand is too challenging). *Practice single-digit addition until your child is fluent prior to working on double-digit addition.*
- Offering a choice of tasks (to follow the individual's MO to the degree possible). *Allow the student to choose what to count, or whether to count or add.*
- Offering a choice of order of tasks (to follow the individual's MO). *Allow the student to choose what order to complete tasks.*
- Varying demands (to prevent satiation with the task). *Do counting one day, adding another day, and sequencing the next.*
- Removing aversive qualities of the task (to decrease MO for escape/avoidance). *If the student does not like to be touched, use gestural prompting (e.g., pointing) rather than physical prompting (e.g., hand-over-hand guidance) to indicate the correct response.*

B. **Eliminate the S^D for escape or avoidance** (i.e., the stimulus that prompts the student's behavior) by:
   - Completing the task in a new setting. *Work outside at a picnic table.*
   - Changing task materials. *Use blocks instead of tokens for counting.*
   - Changing the wording used for the task. *Instead of saying, "Let's count the ladybugs," try, "How many ladybugs are crawling on our picnic blanket?"*
   - Changing people involved with the task. *Switch instructors. Consider having peers give instruction to one another with a parent or professional facilitating.*

C. **Add predictability to the demand** by:
   - Preparing the individual for the upcoming demand. *Tell the student, "Counting is coming up next."*

- Letting the individual know exactly what will be required. *Tell the student, "We will count trucks and racecars, and then we will be done."*
- Helping the individual see where the demand fits in the day's routine. *Use an activity schedule to indicate when the task will be coming up and what will follow. Try to have a preferred activity follow a challenging or nonpreferred demand. A sample schedule might alternate between a challenging academic task, a preferred task, and a social task.*

Step 3: Replacement Skill

Choose one or more of the strategies below to teach a **replacement skill.** An illustration of each strategy follows in italics.

A. **Teach the individual to make an appropriate request for a break.** *Teach an adult with autism to sign for a break. Be sure to reinforce appropriate behavior immediately at first.*

   Note: Even speaking individuals with autism may need practice requesting a break or ending a task appropriately. Just because someone can physically ask for a break does not mean that she will do it. The only way to ensure that your child or student will "use her words" is to prompt the person to ask for what she wants, when she wants it, and to reinforce this request immediately. For example, if a group home staff member asks a resident to do the dishes and she says, "I'd rather not," this statement must be honored if we want it to replace a more serious behavior. She can be taught to delay gratification and accept "no" at a later time, once she has a fluent requesting repertoire. Alternatively, if a resident really hates doing the dishes, maybe she can be assigned to cook or do laundry instead.

B. **Teach the individual to communicate that she will do something later.** *Teach an adult with autism to sign, "Later." Be sure to reinforce immediately at first and systematically introduce a delay to reinforcement. See note above regarding the need for immediate reinforcement.*

C. **Teach the individual how to put demands in an order.** That is, if the person needs to do several tasks but the order of completion is not important, let her select the order. *Use a picture schedule with*

Velcro-backed pictures so that the individual can select the order. Be sure to reinforce her.

D. **Teach the skills needed to tolerate a demand.** *Teach an adult to listen to music on headphones while completing vocational responsibilities to make the task more palatable to her. Teach a child to find the answers to challenging homework questions in her notes.*

E. **Teach endurance and build tolerance.** *If an adult is beginning a job in the laundry room of a hotel, require her to fold only one towel at first, and then gradually and systematically increase her rate to the amount required by the job. If a child has difficulty staying near others to work in a group at school, gradually have her move closer to the group while she works.*

Step 4: Consequence-based Strategy

Choose one or more of the **consequence-based strategies below.**

A. **Use one of the types of reinforcement** discussed in Chapter 4 (DRA, DRI, DRH). *Provide an adolescent with a three-minute walk through the hall each time she makes an appropriate request rather than arguing with the teacher to escape the classroom. Consider using a DRH to systematically increase the amount of classroom participation required to earn reinforcement. Similarly, a child who gets out of her seat at dinner to escape the demand of eating might be reinforced for taking a designated number of bites by being allowed to leave the table.*

B. **Use an extinction procedure** to ensure that problem behaviors no longer lead to escaping the task. *If a student yells in class to escape the class work and is typically taken to time out, bring the student out of the room to prevent further disruption, but have her complete the class work in the hallway.*

C. **Use a punishment** to ensure that the problem behavior will result in a response that will discourage the individual from doing the behavior in the future. For example, a student who makes wisecracks in math class in order to try to escape doing long division might earn an extra division problem to solve for each wisecrack.

Ideas for Addressing Behaviors Maintained by Attention

Step 1: Clarify Understanding of the Function of the Behavior

Be sure that you know:

- What type of attention does the individual want? Consider:
    - ❑ High intensity versus low intensity (e.g., loud praise as opposed to quiet praise; big squeezes as opposed to gentle hugs, etc.)
    - ❑ Solo versus divided (getting complete attention from one person versus attention from someone who is repeatedly distracted by another person or social demand)
    - ❑ Group versus individual (being one of a larger number of people interacting with someone versus being alone with someone)
    - ❑ Emotional versus neutral (attention delivered with an animated face, voice, and gestures, versus attention delivered with less expression)
    - ❑ Physical versus vocal versus nonverbal (e.g., does she want hugs? praise? a smile?)
- Who does the individual want attention from?
- Is the individual attempting to regain a certain quality of attention or avoid loss of a certain quality of attention? (For example, when she has eaten alone, has she learned that throwing food will get someone's attention, or has she learned that throwing food is a surefire way to keep a preferred person nearby?)
- How long can the person tolerate low levels of attention?

Step 2: Antecedent Strategies

Choose one or more of the **antecedent strategies** from the list below. An illustration of each strategy follows in italics.

A. **Prepare the individual for upcoming changes in the level of attention,** and provide clear expectations of how long the attention level will be changed. *Tell a group home resident, "I need to take care of a couple of things. I will be back before lunch starts." Or, tell a young child that you will put on her favorite TV show (e.g., a 10-minute "Little Bear" episode) while you make a phone call, and when the show ends, it will be time to play with Mommy again.*

B. **Direct the individual to do a specific activity** during the period of altered attention. *Redirect a group home resident to a preferred art activity during a period of low attention. Consider giving a younger child a puzzle, a page to color, or a snack. Sometimes an automatic bubble blower, a lava lamp, or snow globe that only comes out when distraction is needed may be helpful for children with fewer independent play skills.*

C. **Schedule desired attention for the individual** to prevent her from reaching the threshold for occurrence of the problem behavior. *For an adult who tolerates low attention for 15 minutes, provide scheduled attention every 10 minutes.*

D. If attention is being decreased or withheld while the individual completes a task, **tell her exactly what she must do to regain the attention she wants.** *Tell a group home resident, "Finish making your bed and then you and I can go for a walk together." Or show a student exactly how many problems she must complete prior to chatting with the teacher again. To this end, a token chart may be useful.*

E. **Keep activities interactive** when possible. *Assign to an adult who is motivated by attention a job that involves social interaction, such as handing out or collecting items, or finding out what fellow residents would like to have for lunch. Assign a child at school an interactive job such as tutoring a younger or less able child, or delivering treats to peers in a special education setting at designated intervals.*

Step 3: Replacement Skills

Choose one or more of the **replacement skills** from the list below. An illustration of each strategy follows in italics.

A. **Teach the individual to make an appropriate request for attention.** *Teach a preschooler with autism to ask her mother to hang up the phone, rather than using a tantrum to regain her mother's attention.*

B. **Teach the individual an appropriate response that will lead to attention.** *Teach a preschooler with autism to take attendance each morning to get attention from peers. She can also be taught to play hand games, give high-fives, tell jokes, or make compliments.*

C. **Teach the individual the skills needed to tolerate less attention.** *Teach a child with autism to look through a photo album while she waits for the teacher to come back to the classroom.*

D. **Teach endurance.** *Provide reinforcement to a student for systematically increasing the amount of time she is able to go without one-to-one attention.*

Step 4: Consequence-based Strategies

Choose one or more of the **consequence-based strategies** from the list below. An illustration of each strategy follows in italics.

A. **Use one of the types of reinforcement** discussed in Chapter 5. *To help a child with autism tolerate lower levels of attention, give her the exact type of attention that maintains the problem behavior (e.g., high intensity attention) when she is not engaging in the problem behavior. If parents and teachers typically respond to the problem behavior with a physical restraint, then reinforce the child's appropriate behavior with bear hugs and wrestling holds.*

B. **Use an extinction procedure** to ensure that problem behaviors no longer lead to attention. *For example, a student I worked with used to blow his nose on his teachers as a means of obtaining attention. To place this behavior on extinction, we ceased responding to this behavior at all. We continued as if it never happened, and eventually the behavior disappeared.*

C. **Use a punishment procedure** to reduce the likelihood that the person will persist in the behavior in the future. *Put a student with autism in Time Out for engaging in the problem behavior, removing her from the attention that she is seeking.*

Ideas for Addressing Behaviors Maintained by Access to Preferred Items and Activities

Step 1: Clarify Understanding of the Function of the Behavior

Be sure that you know:
- What type of item/activity does the individual want? Consider:
    - ❏ Is it food? If so, is it salty foods? Sweet foods? Mushy foods? Cold foods? etc.
    - ❏ Is it a drink? If so, is it cold? Sweet? etc.
    - ❏ Is it something to listen to? Is it loud? Soft? Musical? Voices? Rhythmic? Melodic?
    - ❏ Is it something to touch? Is it sticky? Squishy? Cold? Warm? Wet?
    - ❏ Is it something to look at? Does it involve lights? Colors? Contrast?
    - ❏ Is it something to smell? What scent?
    - ❏ Is it an activity? Is it high energy? Does it involve a certain sensation? Does it involve a cognitive challenge?
    - ❏ Does it involve creating something? Is paint preferred? Crayons? Glue? Play-Doh?
    - ❏ Note: It is important to come up with groups of specific items/activities that the person desires so you can ensure that these types of items or activities are used as reinforcers for appropriate behavior.
- Is the individual attempting to regain a certain item/activity or avoid the loss of it?
- Is it a problem for the individual to give up the item/activity, wait for the item/activity, or share the item/activity?
- How long can the individual go without access to this item/activity before engaging in the problem behavior?

Step 2: Antecedent Strategies

Choose one or more of the **antecedent strategies** from the list below. An illustration of each strategy follows in italics.

A. **Give the person access to desired items/activities throughout the day** to the extent possible. *For a child with autism who is interested in Dr. Seuss books, use Dr. Seuss books for reading programs and use Dr. Seuss games to work on turn-taking skills. Create math word problems using Dr. Seuss characters, and use sentences about events in Dr. Seuss books for spelling tests. Be sure to intersperse other preferred materials with the Dr. Seuss content to prevent satiation. For inclusion classrooms, consider incorporating varied popular topics throughout the day, with the student with autism's special topic mixed in daily.*

B. **When the items/activities will not be available, try to incorporate competing reinforcers** (other things the individual might want). *Provide preferred snacks or a preferred craft activity during social studies, when Dr. Seuss material cannot be incorporated.*

C. **Schedule access to preferred items/activities at intervals shorter than a student's threshold for the problem behavior.** *For a student who can go 30 minutes without access to a preferred item or activity, provide scheduled access every 20 minutes.*

D. **Use schedules or other cues to alert the individual that a time is coming when she will have to give up or share the item or activity.** *A teacher might announce, "In one minute, book time will be over." At home, a parent might say, "When the big hand is on the 5, it will be your brother's turn to hold the remote."*

E. **Use schedules or other cues to let the individual know when or how she can get access to the desired items/activities.** *A teacher might post a schedule on the board in the classroom, then point to that schedule and say, "We will work on science projects for three more minutes, and then it will be book time." At home, when your child is constantly pestering you for chips, you might use a picture schedule to indicate after which activities the chips will be available.*

F. **Offer frequent choices** of desired activities and items throughout the day. *A teacher might offer choices of materials to be used for different projects, choices of centers in the classroom, etc. Offering choices helps take the guesswork out of identifying the individual's current Motivating Operations.*

Step 3: Replacement Skills

Choose one or more of the **replacement skills** from the list below. An illustration of each strategy follows in italics.

A. **Teach the individual an appropriate request** for preferred items and activities. *Teach a nonverbal adult with autism to use the Picture Exchange Communication System (Bondy & Frost, 1985) to make requests at work.*

B. **Teach the individual with autism how to independently get access** to preferred items and activities. *Teach an adult with autism to pack a bag of preferred items to bring to work and to go get those items on his or her break. Have your child keep her favorite items in her pocket, as long as they do not distract her from work.*

C. **Teach waiting skills.** *Teach an adult with autism to wait increasingly long periods of time for a requested item. This waiting program can begin with having the adult wait a few seconds for an object in view. The waiting time can be gradually and systematically increased so the person is waiting for an extended period of time with the object placed out of sight. The reinforcer for this program should be a heavy dose of whatever the adult initially requested.*

D. **Teach the individual to tolerate "no."** Begin by saying "no" to requests that will be easier to accept, and systematically progress to saying "no" to a highly motivated request. You may need to create a hierarchy of refusals that range from easy to difficult for the person to accept. *Give an alternative, highly preferred object or activity to a student with autism immediately, provided she accepts "no" without any problem behaviors. For example, if the student asks to go out for pizza, and you say no, you can give her pretzels (another preferred snack) to show your appreciation for her graceful acceptance of your refusal to take her for pizza.*

   Note: *Say "yes" to requests whenever possible, even once the individual can tolerate "no" well. The goal of teaching someone to tolerate "no" is not to decrease her quality of life by having her accept "no" all the time. Instead, you are ensuring that when the individual really needs to accept "no" (e.g., she is requesting to watch television when it is time to go to work), she will not react with the problem behavior.*

E. **Teach the skill of making a second choice.** Offer a preferred "second choice" to an individual who cannot be given her first choice. Provide her with heavy doses of the second-choice item and praise her for "making a second choice" or "finding something else." This program may be implemented according to a hierarchy as with the "tolerating no" program, above. *Begin by offering your child the things she prizes most when she can't have her first choice and gradually start offering her less preferred (but still enjoyable) activities or items.*

F. **Teach sharing.** Begin by asking a child with autism to share something that she does not particularly care about. *For example, give your child two napkins at dinner and ask her to "share" one with the person next to her.* Reinforce her for sharing with a highly preferred item/activity. Gradually and systematically increase the demands of sharing until the child does not have difficulty sharing the item that had previously led to the problem behavior—although she is perhaps only sharing for a few seconds. Again, a hierarchy might be helpful.

G. **Teach the individual to give items back.** Beginning with non-preferred items, have the individual hand you items that she has or is close to. *For example, ask your child to hand you the salt on the table, or a tissue.* Provide her with a highly preferred item or activity to reinforce her for giving you items you request. Gradually and systematically increase the demands of giving back items until the person does not have any difficulty giving back the item that had previously led to the problem behavior. Again, a hierarchy might be helpful.

H. **Teach turn-taking.** Begin with simple turn-taking games. *For young children, consider games that focus on turn taking only, such as "Don't Break the Ice" (Hasbro), "Crocodile Dentist" (Winning Moves), "Honeybee Tree" (International Playthings), etc. For students who have matching skills, consider playing "Memory" (Hasbro) with the cards face up so that the individual will have to match rather than remember, "Cariboo" (Cranium), or "Candy Land" (Milton Bradley). Individuals with more advanced skills can select from a wider array of turn-taking games based on their interests.*

The important thing is to find an activity that the individual with autism really enjoys. Be creative. For someone who loves music, take turns playing tunes on the piano. Once the person can take turns in a motivating context, introduce items and activities that will need to be passed along or given up as the individual's "turn." This will help to prepare the individual for the fact that she will need to give up the item or stop the activity, but will be allowed access to them at some point again.

Step 4: Consequence-based Strategies

If you have decided to try a **consequence-based strategy,** choose one or more of the strategies below. An illustration of each strategy follows in italics.

A. **Try one of the reinforcement strategies** discussed in Chapter 4 (DRA, DRI, DRH). Reinforce all replacement skills. *For example, if you are teaching your child or student with autism to raise her hand rather than calling out, initially reinforce her whenever she raises her hand.*

B. **Use an extinction procedure** to ensure that problem behaviors no longer lead to preferred items/activities. *For example, if your child has gotten attention in the past for calling out, ignore her when she calls out.* Note: There are two situations where using extinction to teach someone not to use a problem behavior to request preferred items/activities becomes confusing:

  1. **Redirection.** Sometimes parents and professionals believe they are redirecting someone to distract her from a challenging behavior when, in fact, the behavior is actually a request for the activity that the person is being redirected to (as with the example of Anthony hitting his head to obtain beads in the Introduction). For extinction to occur, this redirection must be stopped.

  2. **Sensory Integration.** Sometimes people with autism are directed to a sensory integration activity with the aim of calming them, when the problem behavior is actually a means of requesting the sensory input. To extinguish the behavior, the sensory activities should be provided before the problem behavior occurs, on a noncontingent schedule, rather than as a consequence for the problem behavior.

C. **Use a punishment procedure** to decrease the likelihood that the person will engage in the problem behavior in the future. For example, take away the student's access to the preferred item/activity if she engages in the problem behavior. A "response cost" works well in this scenario. This involves stipulating that a certain amount of the item/activity is lost as a consequence for the problem behavior. *For example, the student loses a certain number of minutes of television, a certain number of treats, or a certain amount of time playing a computer game CD.* You may recall Darra's mother using this strategy in the Introduction when she took away minutes of television each time Darra spoke of Clay. This strategy was ineffective, though, because it was not matched to the function of Darra's constant talking about Clay Aiken.

Ideas for Addressing Behaviors Maintained by Automatic Reinforcement

Step 1: Clarify Understanding of the Function of the Behavior

Be sure that you know:

A. Exactly what type of stimulation does the individual want? Consider:

- Visual, hearing, tactile, smell, taste, movement?
- Intense or gentle?
- Pain reduction? Inducement of a pleasurable feeling?
- Some kind of mental stimulation or calming of emotions?

It is important to identify the specific sensory input so that you can provide it to the individual in a very controlled manner, or you can identify an appropriate alternative.

Step 2: Antecedent Strategies

Choose one or more of the antecedent strategies below. An illustration of each follows in italics.

A. **Make sure that the individual with autism always has direction** as to what she should be doing. This will decrease the MO for automatically reinforcing behaviors that the person might use to fill her time. *To keep your student with autism from hand-flapping while you gather materials for instruction, give her a puzzle to complete.*

B. **Make sure that what the student is directed to do is stimulating enough to compete with the automatic reinforcement behaviors.** If she is involved in a reinforcing, stimulating activity, she will have a diminished MO to engage in an automatic reinforcement behavior. At school, *use a structured assessment tool, such as the ABLLS (Sundberg & Partington, 1998) to develop an appropriately challenging curriculum, and teach the curriculum using a quick pace and preferred materials. At home, keep a box of preferred activities and snacks that you only make available to your child when she needs to keep herself occupied.*

C. **Rule out illnesses or injuries.** Especially if your child or student is not very verbal, she may use behavior to communicate pain or discomfort. *If a student with autism suddenly starts biting objects, take her to the dentist; if she starts head banging, take her to the doctor to see if she has an ear infection.*

D. **Teach the individual a cue** that lets her know when the automatic reinforcement activity is or is not acceptable. *Teach a student with autism that she can run along the fence when she sees the green traffic light, but not the red.*

E. **Provide free access to similar, but appropriate activities** that might satisfy the motivation for the original activity. *For a student who enjoys rocking, provide a rocking chair. For a student who enjoys jumping, provide a trampoline. For a student who enjoys humming, provide a microphone with companion headphones for the student to hear herself.*

F. **Provide free access to the automatic reinforcement activity in a certain place.** In other words, establish "stimulus control"—a place, time, or situation where a certain activity is permissible. *Create a "talking chair" in a child's bedroom where self-talk is allowed. Create a "tearing pile" of paper for a student who tears things up. Direct a student who is masturbating publicly to her bathroom at home.*

Step 3: Replacement Skills

Choose one of the **replacement skills** described below. An illustration of each strategy follows in italics.

A. **Teach the individual an appropriate way of requesting the "stimulus control" area.** *Teach a teenager with autism to excuse herself to go to the bathroom to masturbate. Teach Darra to only speak about Clay to her mother at a certain time of day.*

B. **Teach waiting skills.** Teach the individual to wait until engaging in the desired automatic reinforcing behavior. Gradually and systematically increase the waiting time. The reinforcer for this program should be uninterrupted access to the automatic reinforcement activity. *For example, if a student waits throughout her two-hour work session to be allowed privacy to masturbate, then she can be given 20 minutes alone as a reinforcer.*

Step 4: Consequence-based Strategies

Choose one or more of the **consequence-based** strategies below. An illustration of each strategy follows in italics.

A. **Use one of the reinforcement strategies discussed in Chapter 4.** Reinforce the student for waiting to engage in the automatic reinforcement behavior with uninterrupted access to the activity. Consider using an alternative, highly preferred item or activity to reinforce lower rates of the automatic reinforcement response (DRL), or the absence of the response (DRO). *For example, for a student who flaps her hands, provide a reinforcer either for lower rates of hand flapping or for the absence of flapping following a certain period of time.*

B. **Try extinction** only with the assistance of a Board Certified Behavior Analyst experienced in behavior intervention. Extinction is extremely challenging to implement for an automatic reinforcement behavior. If attempted without expert guidance, the intervention might be ineffective, or overly intrusive for the individual.

C. **Choose possible punishment procedures with care.** Because the reinforcer is not under external control, it cannot be taken away contingent upon the problem behavior. That is, the person herself controls the sensation that she gets when she flaps her hands, rocks her body, or bangs her head. No outside person can take away the sensations she feels when she engages in the problem behavior. Therefore, positive and negative punishment for automatic reinforcement behaviors must be unrelated to the function of the behavior. *A response cost system might be implemented in which a small amount of a privilege is taken away whenever the person engages in the automatic reinforcement behavior. Or, a mild reprimand or other response that the person finds aversive might be used.*

Strategies to Enhance Any Intervention Plan

There are some strategies that may be used in conjunction with any of the above strategies and may enhance their effectiveness when targeting problem behaviors in children and adults with autism spectrum disorders. These strategies are discussed below:

Rule Cards

Most of us engage in some behaviors solely because we know the "rules." In other words, we don't have to learn what happens if we do or don't follow the rules by experience. We know the consequences of certain actions because someone has told us about them. For example, most of us wouldn't dream of trying to drive 100 mph in a 55 mph zone, because we know that we could easily crash or get a speeding ticket if we did. Likewise, when we start a new job, we know that if we come to work and do as our boss tells us, we will get a paycheck and a certain amount of vacation time.

Using rule cards, presented either in words or pictorially, can help individuals with autism learn contingencies. For example, to let a student with autism know that she will be reinforced for being quiet while the teacher reads a story, a teacher might give her a card with a picture of a face with a finger to the lips followed by a picture of the desired reward. Students who can read may be given written rules.

Self-monitoring and Self-management

Research suggests that when students monitor and regulate their own behavior, the intervention plan is likely to be slightly more effective (e.g., Bolstad & Johnston, 1972). Furthermore, self-management ensures that a person who can provide consequences for the individual's behavior is always present (since the individual is taught to give herself reinforcement or punishment). In addition, when a child or student with autism can use self-management techniques, it reduces the demands on a parent's or professional's time. Self-management and self-monitoring can be used to implement almost any intervention.

See Chapter 5 for more information on self-monitoring and self-management.

Keep It Simple Summary

Use the menu of strategies presented in this chapter to create an intervention package customized for your individual student or child and the function of his or her problem behavior. Be sure that your package includes:

■ at least one antecedent strategy,
■ at least one replacement skill, and
■ at least one consequence-based intervention.

7 | Managing Special Considerations

When creating behavior intervention plans for individuals with autism or other developmental disabilities, there are some situations that require special consideration. In these cases, there are variables that might make an otherwise effective approach ineffective. For example, your child or student might have a problem behavior that serves more than one function or he might experience a traumatic event during the time that a behavior intervention plan is being implemented. Knowing what variables to look for, and having a general concept of how to respond, will allow you to create effective interventions in the face of these potential obstacles.

Behaviors that Serve More than One Function

Some problem behaviors serve more than one function at a time. For example, Riley, a 7-year-old boy with Asperger's disorder, sometimes threw chairs when he was in his inclusive classroom at school. A functional assessment revealed that this behavior served two purposes: 1) to allow him to escape from the school work (which he found too easy), and 2) to obtain peer attention (which he had trouble getting appropriately). Addressing Riley's behavior was a challenge because sending him out of the classroom was a reinforcer, since it allowed him to escape from the work he perceived to be boring. By the same token, keeping him in the classroom was a reinforcer too, since his chair-throwing attracted intense attention from his classmates.

In cases like Riley's, there are no simple answers. Only through creative planning can you avoid inadvertently reinforcing the problem behavior. For Riley, the following strategies were incorporated:

- Riley's teacher organized cooperative learning groups to provide Riley with peer attention before he threw chairs.
- Riley's teacher created a folder of enrichment activities for Riley to complete independently if the class work seemed too easy for him.
- Riley was taught to appropriately ask to leave the room to go see a favorite guidance counselor.
- If Riley threw a chair, he was, by necessity, asked to leave the room (as his behavior was distracting and dangerous to peers). However, all of the work being discussed in class was brought to the principal's office and he was required to complete it there. He was then not allowed to complete enrichment activities, only the "boring" work.
- A rule book was provided to inform Riley of the possible rewards and punishments for his behavior.
- At the end of each day that Riley did not throw chairs, he was permitted to stand in front of the class and tell the "joke of the day," which typically led to intense attention from his classmates.
- At the end of each week that Riley did not throw chairs, Riley was invited to go to a kindergarten class and read the children a book, which also led to a great deal of attention.
- Riley received social skills training which continued to target appropriate ways to obtain and maintain peer attention.

By thinking Riley's problem behavior through carefully, his team members successfully met the challenges of a behavior serving multiple functions. The general strategies that were used to address Riley's behavior are the same ones that will likely be effective in addressing your child's or student's problem behaviors that serve more than one function:

- Select antecedents that will prevent the occurrence of the problem behavior as much as possible.

- Teach replacement behaviors for the problem behaviors (e.g., requesting to speak to the guidance counselor).
- Make sure that the consequences for appropriate behavior earn your child or student more reinforcers than the problem behavior does.

You may also be able to avoid the reinforcing consequences for the problem behavior that the individual is used to receiving. For example, in Riley's case, both escape and peer attention for the problem behavior were avoided.

Many Behaviors That Serve the Same Function

Some people with autism use multiple behaviors that all serve the same function. For example, you may recall reading about Amos, who hit and pinched teachers when he was not allowed access to his preferred items or activities. Hitting and pinching both served the same function for Amos.

In this kind of situation, where someone uses several different behaviors to accomplish the same thing, you can use the strategy menu in the previous chapter as if it were just one behavior serving that function. When you have thoroughly addressed the function of that one behavior, all related behaviors should decrease. As with the example of Amos, all behaviors serving the same function will be affected together. However, be sure to collect data on all of the problem behaviors to ensure that no unexpected changes occur.

If the individual uses different behaviors in response to different people or things in the environment (different discriminative stimuli), then be sure to consider each individual S^D in creating the intervention plan. For example, if a student with autism hits one particular teacher to escape tasks, but flops on the floor for another teacher, be sure to include both behaviors in the plan, as well as antecedent strategies specific to each teacher.

Reinforcer Substitution

Sometimes a behavior starts out serving one function, but eventually comes to serve a different function. In other words, the behavior was initially reinforced by one consequence, but, over time, it starts to be reinforced by a different consequence. One reinforcer has substituted for another.

Ezra, a 9-year-old boy with autism, had a behavior problem that provides a clear example of reinforcer substitution. Ezra did a great deal of spitting. Functional assessment data revealed that Ezra spat because he enjoyed watching the spit's trajectory. In other words, spitting initially served an automatic reinforcement function for Ezra.

Ezra's team introduced a slight punishment as a consequence for spitting. Specifically, Ezra was taught to stop what he was doing and wipe up the spit. At first, this consequence effectively reduced the spitting. However, Ezra soon realized that if he spat during an activity he did not enjoy, he would have to wipe the spit up, which would delay the task. Unfortunately, some of Ezra's tasks were less enjoyable to him than wiping up spit. During these tasks, Ezra began to spit nearly continuously. Between spitting and cleaning, he would run out of time in the teaching session and completely avoid unwanted tasks. At this point, spitting was no longer serving an automatic reinforcement function for Ezra. It was now serving an escape function for him.

If you closely monitor your interventions, you will know right away if the problem behavior begins to increase. This might be a sign that reinforcer substitution has occurred. Use the troubleshooting strategies described in Chapter 10 to help determine the reasons why a behavior has increased. If reinforcer substitution is the culprit, you will need to modify your intervention. For Ezra, the plan was changed so that his teachers ignored his spitting, he was given tasks that were less challenging and more interesting to him, and he was allowed to spray water into the sink on a rich, noncontingent schedule. These modifications were enough to eliminate Ezra's spitting behavior.

To summarize, if, during the course of your behavior plan, the problem behavior takes on a new function, you must identify the new function, and start over in developing a behavior plan that addresses the new function.

A Successful Intervention Interrupted by Illness or Stress

Sometimes, an intervention is running along smoothly, but then the person with an autism spectrum disorder becomes sick or experiences a stressful event. In this case, people often ask whether or not to proceed with the intervention.

This question must be answered on an individual basis. Although your initial instinct may be to "lighten up" on your child or student, this may not always be the best choice. Consider the research finding (Dozier et al., 2007) mentioned in Chapter 5 that children actually preferred having a behavioral treatment over not having one. Consider, too, that parenting literature has long emphasized that children prefer caregivers who set limits as opposed to those who are wholly permissive. In fact, keeping a behavior plan in place might actually be less stressful for people with autism and related disorders than temporarily suspending or removing the plan.

With that said, in some cases it might be appropriate to slightly modify the plan, as you might in response to a known setting event. For example, you might choose to place fewer demands in a row on your child or student, or shorten the delay before you provide reinforcement. If you decide to make changes along these lines, then be sure to communicate the changes in writing to all team members to make sure that everyone responds to the individual's behaviors the same way.

Implementing Behavior Interventions in a Group

It can be challenging to carry out an individualized behavior intervention plan in a group or public setting. First, it can be difficult to implement the plan discreetly. And second, in a group, your resources may be stretched so it is harder to give individualized attention to the person with the problem behavior. Parents and teachers of students in inclusive classrooms, in particular, often have questions about overcoming this type of challenge.

Using Interventions That Benefit All Group Members

When planning a behavioral intervention to use in a group setting, the first question to consider is: Will the whole group benefit from the intervention components, or just the individual?

You should consider using the intervention with the whole group, so as not to single out the person with autism for the intervention.

More often than not, the whole group will benefit. Consider Riley, for example. His chair-throwing was related in part to work that he perceived to be "boring." As part of his behavior plan, he was given access to enrichment work. In reality, every student in his class would have benefited from that option. Although not every student would *need* to go above and beyond the curriculum, every student would benefit from the *availability* of this work. Chances are, if one student is bored, other students are bored too. The difference is simply that the student with autism lacks the social skills to hide his boredom.

Although certain interventions might only be *necessary* for one individual in a group, they may be harmless, and even beneficial for all group members. The list of possible helpful interventions is endless. The following list is a sample of some components of interventions that can be easily and helpfully implemented in an inclusive setting:

- Form cooperative learning groups (provides peer attention).
- Call on students when their hands are not raised (provides teacher attention, increases engagement and consequently decreases all functions of a student's off-task behaviors).
- Individualize the complexity of questions that students are asked (adjusts the level of challenge of a task, which increases engagement for students and consequently decreases all functions of students' off-task behaviors).
- Incorporate students' favorite topics or materials into the curriculum (e.g., give the class math word problems about pop stars). Note: When an individual's favorite topics are mixed together with other topics popular among the students, no one will know that specific topics were chosen for one particular student (pairs tasks with reinforcement).
- Write instructions on the board, or break down complex tasks into steps written on the board (adjusts the level of challenge of a task, which increases engagement and consequently decreases all functions of off-task behaviors).
- Provide class-wide rewards for certain behaviors or accomplishments, such as earning a pizza party if all students meet a challenge set by the teacher (e.g., finish a complex project by a certain date) (students prompt and reinforce one another toward the goal, resulting in peer attention; pairs on-task behaviors with reinforcement).

■ Establish teams in the classroom and have them jointly earn points toward rewards—for instance, by allowing teams to earn a homework pass for following instructions, task completion, and class participation (students prompt and reinforce one another toward the goal, resulting in peer attention; pairs on-task behaviors with reinforcement).

■ Create explicit, class-wide expectations, rules, and reinforcement systems related to accepting differences, being kind to classmates, and including classmates (increases culture of acceptance of the student with autism, pairs the teaching environment with reinforcement, increases positive peer attention, and increases peer receptiveness to attempts by the student with autism to interact appropriately).

This above list of ideas is by no means exhaustive, but is instead meant to trigger ideas of how to adapt components of behavior plans for individuals so that they benefit larger groups. For more information on setting class-wide expectations, and even school-wide expectations, read the summary by Robert Horner and George Sugai (2005) about school-wide positive behavior intervention and support practices, or visit the Positive Behavior Intervention and Support website: www.pbis.org/main.htm.

Sometimes, people with autism and related disorders are included in groups where many other individuals also have challenging behaviors and need support. A special education classroom provides a common example of this type of setting, as does a group home. For these settings, more explicit group contingencies (consequences for both appropriate and inappropriate behaviors) are often successful.

A "level system" provides one example of an explicit group contingency. In a level system, doing specified appropriate behaviors (such as completing assignments or participating in class) allows an individual to move up a level in a hierarchy of privileges, and doing specified inappropriate behaviors sends the individual down a level in a hierarchy of privileges.

For example, a classroom might have various levels. At the highest level, students might be able to select from a variety of books, games, and crafts during indoor recess. They might be able to choose their own enrichment activities if they complete their work quickly enough. They might have less homework than their peers. In contrast, students at the lowest level might have only limited activities during recess, and may not be able to get up from their seats during work. Additionally, they would have to complete all of their homework. Each successively higher level allows the individual access to increased privileges and reinforcers. (See Smith & Farrell, 1993, listed in the References, for more information.)

A level system is often helpful for a group with many behavioral needs, because both group and individualized behavior goals and reinforcers can be plugged into it.

Using Interventions That Benefit Just One Member of a Group

Not every group that includes an individual with autism or another disability will benefit from a group intervention, and some interventions are not feasible to do in a group. In these cases, it is important to create individualized interventions that minimize both stigmatization of the person with the challenging behavior and loss of resources from the rest of the group. Again, for this challenge, there are no simple answers, but awareness and creativity can lead to sensible intervention. Below is another list of sample strategies to consider. While not exhaustive, the list is intended to help trigger ideas for specific situations you may encounter.

- Establish a coded warning signal for the individual, such as pulling down the first window shade for strike one, the second for strike two, etc.
- Place a Post-it note describing appropriate behaviors in the individual's book, on his desk, or with his work supplies.
- Teach self-monitoring or self-management (see Chapter 5).
- Keep materials (e.g., enrichment folder, behavior chart, reinforcers) with the person's task materials so that he may use them independently and discreetly.
- Remind others nearby (in earshot of the individual with autism) of the instructions or the rules so that it is not obvious to others that he is the one who needs to be reminded of the rules.
- Pull the person with autism aside before an activity to review the rules or instructions.

- Discreetly flash an index card with a visual prompt, such as a "shh" sign, on it.
- Carry a small notepad in your pocket to keep track of points or other tokens the individual has earned toward reinforcement. Subtly show the page to the individual.

Again, the ideas above are by no means exhaustive, but are meant to trigger ideas for "undercover" behavior management.

8 | Measuring the Effectiveness of Your Behavior Plan

Once your behavior plan is in place, you will undoubtedly want to be sure it is working. You have worked so hard to this point to ensure that the problem behavior actually will change. The key to guaranteeing a successful intervention is ongoing measurement. You probably selected a measurement strategy during your functional assessment. You will continue to use this strategy throughout your intervention to allow you to compare apples to apples, so to speak. In other words, this comparison will let you know if the problem behavior is any different after the intervention than it was before the intervention.

For assistance in selecting what specifically to measure, see *Functional Behavior Assessment for People with Autism: Making Sense of Seemingly Senseless Behavior.* In that book, you will find specific instructions to help your team decide how to quantify a problem behavior. In this book, you will learn how to use those measurement tools to ensure that your behavior plan will work.

Collecting Baseline Data

The first step in implementing any behavior intervention plan is identifying a "baseline." A baseline paints a picture of the behavior prior to the intervention. It answers the question, "What was the strength of the behavior before we did anything to change it?" In other words, if we never intervened, how often and how intensely would the behavior occur?

The most common myth surrounding baseline data is that you should ignore the problem behavior while you are collecting the data. However, suddenly ignoring a behavior that was not ignored before is, in fact, itself an intervention. The consequences for the behavior will have changed.

Instead, during baseline data collection, continue responding to the behavior just as you normally would. Whatever you were doing before, keep doing it. In my experience, doing what you were doing before often means "winging it," or responding differently every time. It is okay to be inconsistent while you are collecting baseline data. If that is what was occurring before, that is the condition that must remain in place while the baseline data is collected.

In many cases, the team continues the data collection that was started during the functional behavior assessment to ensure a solid and current baseline. In other words, if data were collected as part of the functional assessment, that data can be used as the beginnings of the baseline. This strategy is strongly recommended.

What Information Does Baseline Data Provide?

Baseline data informs us about three critical aspects of the problem behavior:
1. the level,
2. the trend, and
3. the degree of variability.

The Level of the Behavior

The "level" of the behavior refers to the general strength of the problem behavior. This can refer to how often, how quickly, or how intensely a behavior is occurring. Many times, measuring baseline allows a team to see that a behavior is not as intrusive as they once thought. Alternatively, a baseline level can alert a team to the urgency for intervention.

Figure 5 on the next page illustrates a low level behavior. If this graph were measuring a highly intrusive behavior, such as aggression, even this low level would be too high and might call for intervention.

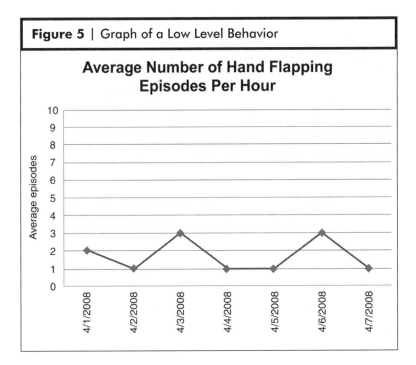

Figure 5 | Graph of a Low Level Behavior

Average Number of Hand Flapping Episodes Per Hour

However, the behavior being measured—hand flapping—has less significant effects, and therefore this level suggests that no intervention is necessary.

The Trend of the Behavior

The "trend" of the behavior refers to the direction in which it is headed. In other words, is the behavior getting stronger, weaker, or staying the same? If a behavior is getting worse or staying at a high level, then an intervention is warranted.

However, sometimes baseline data reveal that a problem behavior is resolving on its own. Whatever environmental variables are currently in place are exactly what is needed for the behavior to go away. In this case, if you change the environment by introducing an intervention, there is a risk that the behavior will instead get stronger.

Occasionally, a behavior might be weakening, but at too slow a pace. In this case, team members may decide that an intervention is worthwhile, all the while acknowledging the risk of derailing the ongoing improvements.

To determine the direction of the behavior you are monitoring, baseline data collection must last long enough to demonstrate patterns of the behavior. The amount of time needed to establish a pattern will differ from case to case. That is why continuing the data collected during the FBA is always a wise choice. Figure 6 illustrates a behavior that is increasing. If this represents an undesireable behavior, then an intervention would certainly be warranted.

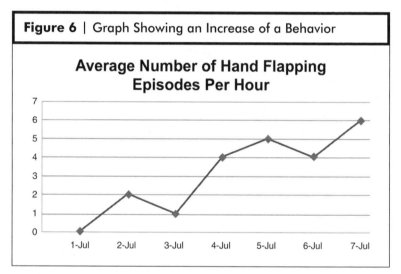

Figure 6 | Graph Showing an Increase of a Behavior

The Variability of the Behavior

The variability of a behavior refers to how it changes from moment to moment. If the behavior stays at a pretty consistent level or follows a pretty consistent growth curve, then the team can be assured that variables that affect the behavior are consistent across settings. If the behavior is variable, meaning that it is sometimes very strong and sometimes very weak, then that gives us a clue that something specific to certain settings or contexts is affecting the behavior. To use an everyday example, you might use much more slang at a dinner with friends than you would use when speaking at a conference. Similarly, a student with autism might engage in more problem behaviors in one classroom than in another, or a student with Asperger's disorder might behave differently with some peers than she does in other circumstances.

It can be beneficial to give variable behaviors some time to stabilize before intervening, as it might turn out that when a trend is finally apparent, the behavior is decreasing. Alternatively, if you label the data points, it may reveal information about which elements in which setting are contributing to differences in the behavior. Figure 7 presents an example of variable data.

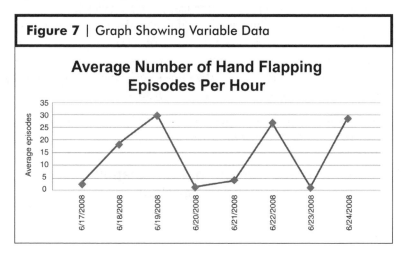

Figure 7 | Graph Showing Variable Data

Collecting Data during the Behavior Intervention

Once a baseline is established, you will be ready to begin intervention. When the intervention is in place, continue collecting the same types of data using the same procedures you used during the baseline period.

You can also use your baseline to help with decision making while you are implementing the behavior plan. You will need to select three different criteria, based on measurement:

1. criteria for reevaluation,
2. fading criteria, and
3. criterion for mastery.

Criteria for Reevaluation

When you set your criteria for reevaluation, you stipulate under what circumstances you will reevaluate your behavior plan. Specifically, you designate a level or rate of increase in the behavior that implies that the plan is not working. The baseline graph can help you to establish this criterion. If you know how to draw a trend line (see Cooper, Heron & Heward, 2007), extrapolate the data out a week or two. If you do not know how to draw an exact trend line, you can use a ruler to estimate the trend line. The trend line will provide an estimate of what the behavior would look like without intervention (see Figure 8, below).

Next, decide how long you would like to give the plan to work. You should base this decision on the severity of the behavior and the complexity of the plan, but do not exceed two weeks. If, by the designated date, the behavior reaches the same level it would have without intervention, then you should reevaluate the plan.

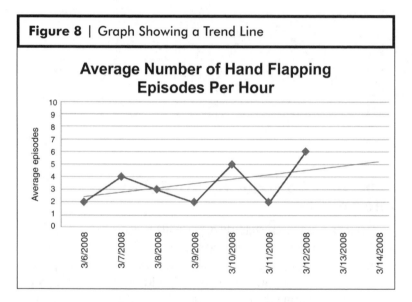

Figure 8 | Graph Showing a Trend Line

Fading Criteria

Next, the plan must include fading criteria so you will know when the individual is doing well enough that the intervention can be lessened. For example, part of an intervention for Emma, who flaps her hands when she wants something to do, might involve immediately reinforcing her for appropriately requesting an activity. One fading step for Emma might include a 5-second delay before providing reinforcement.

Consider establishing fading steps based on a specified percentage decrease in the problem behavior. Also consider establishing a time period that the behavior must remain at a given level before you begin fading the behavior plan. A sample fading criteria might be a 25 percent reduction in the problem behavior maintained across three consecutive days. Remember, not all components of all plans need to be faded. For example, Riley, the student mentioned in Chapter 7 who threw chairs when bored in class, will always need access to enriched academic work to prevent boredom.

Criterion for Mastery

Finally, a criterion for mastery must be established. This specifies at what level the behavior will no longer merit intervention. This criterion will be reached after you have progressed through various steps of fading and after the behavior has been maintained at a given level for a certain period of time.

Dangerous behaviors will likely need to be wholly eliminated. For example, a sample criterion for mastery for Amos, who hit and bit others when he was unable to get access to his preferred items, might be "zero instances of hitting or biting across six months."

In contrast, challenging behaviors that are not dangerous will be tolerable at lower levels. For example, one student my colleague worked with would repeatedly check his answers with his teacher when completing class work. The criterion for mastery for this student was that he could ask one question per assignment.

When setting a criterion for mastery, try to set it at the highest level that will not interfere with the individual's functioning. In other words, a behavior does not have to be eliminated just on principle. It does, however, need to be reduced to a level where it will not cause any harm or interfere with the person's activities or other people's activities. For example, one student I worked with liked to feel different fabrics and might bolt across a room (or a street!) to touch certain fabrics. Ultimately, this student learned to choose a few pieces of cloth each morning to keep in her pocket and feel throughout the day. This brought her behavior to an acceptable level rather than eliminating it.

Graphing Your Data

As you can see from the above sections, a graph is an essential part of a behavior intervention package. It is integral for decision making. Almost every choice you make about the plan should be made while you are looking at the graph of the data. In my experience, the most common obstacle to successful graphing is the belief that your graphs should look perfect. Let that go. A graph needs to be practical and usable rather than attractive. To that end, I recommend the following:

1. Use graph paper and a pencil for all graphs. It takes almost no time at all to place a dot on a piece of paper. Because it requires so little effort, everyone on the team is more likely to graph their own data each day.

2. Ask each team member to graph their own data, and to do so immediately. This will ensure that each team member will see the graph each day, and therefore have a current sense of the trends in the individual's behavior.

3. Train each team member to graph independently, and to read the graph independently. Team members are much more likely to look at the graph and keep it updated if they know what it means. Also, post the decision rules (regarding fading the behavior or reevaluating the behavior plan) on or next to the actual graph.

4. Keep the graph, a pencil, and a ruler (if needed) easily accessible to the team members.

5. To construct a graph, follow these steps:

   a. Take a piece of graph paper.

   b. Label the top with the name of the problem behavior.

   c. Create vertical and horizontal axes by using a ruler to draw a vertical line that intersects with the horizontal line. It should look like two sides of a square.

   d. Label the horizontal axis that you have drawn "date." At each point where a vertical line in the graph paper intersects the horizontal axis, write a date that you will be collecting data. For example, for a school-based plan, write down each school day.

   e. Label the vertical axis with the behavior you are measuring (e.g., "Total hits" or "Head hits per minute"). At each point where a horizontal line in the graph paper intersects the vertical axis, mark off the appropriate unit of measure of the behavior (e.g., total hits, percent of intervals with self-talk episodes, rate of head hits per minute, duration in minutes of tantrums).

f. To graph, place a dot at the intersection between the date and the day's measure of the behavior. (See Figure 9.)

Figure 9 | Hand-drawn Graph

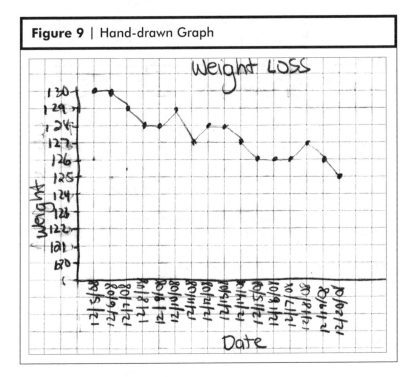

What If Data Show the Plan Is Not Working?

Sometimes, your careful measurement will lead you to discover that your plan is not working. If this occurs, proceed through the following steps:

1. Check treatment integrity. Is the plan being implemented as intended and written? (See Figure 10 for a sample checklist.) In the vast majority of cases, treatment integrity errors are responsible for an unsuccessful plan.

2. If the treatment integrity is good, but the plan continues to be ineffective, reexamine the function of the problem behavior. Did it change? Was it correctly assessed?

3. If the identified function appears correct, reassess whether or not the interventions chosen are actually addressing the function. For example, if a functional assessment reveals that Hannah's toileting accidents are occurring as a means of obtaining attention, then reinforcing her appropriate use of the toilet with a sticker

---

Figure 10 | Sample Checklist for Treatment Integrity

(This sample checklist is for a particular student's problem behavior in the classroom that is maintained by both attention and escape. Each individual's treatment integrity plan must be individualized.)

Instructor:_____ **Date:**_____

Complete this form after each discrete trial teaching session. Indicate yes with a "y" or no with an "n" for each question.

Did I practice each learning goal at least 5 times? _____

Did I present a mix of more and less challenging tasks (including about 25% challenging tasks and 75% less challenging)?_____

Did I praise each correct response? _____

Did I interact in the student's preferred manner (i.e., intensely animated)?

_____

Did I use the natural environment for teaching materials where possible?

_____

Did I roughhouse with the student at least every 2 minutes? _____

Did I capitalize on or create opportunities for peer interaction at least every 10 minutes? _____

Did I use the agreed-upon correction procedure for each error?_____

chart is unlikely to be effective. Furthermore, examine replacement skills to determine if they are at the right level for the individual. Continuing the above example, if Hannah has great difficulty using speech to make requests, it is unreasonable to have her use speech to request using the bathroom as a replacement skill.

If your plan is still not working after you have taken the above steps, refer to Chapter 10 for some additional possible explanations.

9 | Writing Up Your Behavior Intervention Plan

By this point in the book, you have hopefully developed some sensible intervention ideas for the seemingly senseless behaviors that you have been facing. However, you have probably noticed that sensible interventions often have multiple components, and potential critical nuances. Additionally, you know from your background on unlearning theory that consistency will be important if you are to successfully change your child's or student's problem behavior. To further complicate matters, rare is the individual with autism who has only one person on his or her intervention team.

In order to ensure that your hard work and well-crafted interventions are not wasted by incorrect or inconsistent implementation, it is essential to write down exactly what you want your team to do. To simplify this process, and to help you double check that all avenues of intervention have been considered, a behavioral intervention form is provided below. The form at the end of this chapter includes explanations of the various subheadings. Appendix B contains a blank, reproducible form that can be used for actual intervention plans.

Additionally, you may recall from Chapter 5 that no intervention plan can be implemented without obtaining consent from the individual or his guardian. Remember, to truly give consent, the client must understand the proposed plan and its possible risks and benefits, and also feel free to decline consent. Parents and individuals with autism must know that their services will not be affected by refusing to consent. For your convenience, a sample consent form to begin intervention is provided on the next page. You can use this form as a cover letter for the written behavior plan. You are free to reproduce this form and use it to introduce behavior intervention plans to parents and individuals with autism spectrum disorders.

Consent Form for Beginning a Behavior Intervention Plan

To: _____ **Date:** _____

Attached please find a copy of a proposed behavior intervention plan for: _____.

It is hoped that if the attached plan is successful, the benefit will be:_____

_____

_____

_____

However, any behavior intervention plan may have associated risks. The risks associated with this plan are:_____

_____

_____

_____

Please review the plan and let the intervention team leader know if you have any questions.

Team Leader: _____

Team Leader's contact information: _____

Some of the terms and procedures described in the plan may be unfamiliar to you. *Your intervention team leader will sit down with you before you sign this and explain all procedures.* If you still have questions, continue asking them. It is very important that you understand the plan before you sign it. If you disagree with this plan or have concerns, your team will work with you to address these disagreements or concerns. A decision not to sign this form will in no way affect any services that you or your dependent will receive.

I,_____, agree to the attached behavior plan.
   (print name)

_____ _____
          (signature)   (date)

BEHAVIOR INTERVENTION PLAN PROTOCOL FORM
With Explanations

SECTION 1: BACKGROUND AND FUNCTIONAL ASSESSMENT INFORMATION

(For more information on completing this section see page 105, **Functional Behavior Assessment for People with Autism: Making Sense of Seemingly Senseless Behavio**r*.)*

NAME OF STUDENT/CLIENT:_____

INTERVENTION TEAM:

Include everyone who will be participating in intervention, which should include all adults who are likely to be present either when the problem behavior occurs, or when an antecedent strategy might be implemented. This will help to ensure that all relevant parties are trained and privy to important communications about the plan. Note that even if a guardian is unlikely to be present when the problem behavior occurs (e.g., a parent who may not see a school-related behavior), he should always be considered part of the team, should be kept informed, and should be allowed input.

TEAM LEADER(S):

Be sure this person can act as a contact throughout the intervention. Specifically, this person should be reachable by all team members should questions or concerns arise, should be kept informed of any unusual circumstances, and should keep abreast of the data and be responsible for altering the plan if needed.

PROBLEM BEHAVIOR:

Use an "operational definition" of the behavior. In other words, describe the problem behavior in such a way that anyone who sees the behavior would recognize it and distinguish it from other behaviors. This definition should help team members measure and count the behavior.

MEASUREMENT PLAN:

Continue to use the measures selected during baseline to allow continued comparison of the problem behavior before and after intervention.

REASON FOR ADDRESSING BEHAVIOR:

Choose all that apply:

❑ Danger to self   ❑ Danger to others

❑ Risk of property damage   ❑ Stigmatizing

❑ Interferes with own adaptive behaviors (i.e., ability to successfully achieve one's goals, such as making friends or learning)

❑ Interferes with others' adaptive behaviors

❑ Other _____

FUNCTIONAL ASSESSMENT METHODS USED:

*To fill out this section, refer back to the FBA. (See page 104, **Making Sense of Seemingly Senseless Behaviors: Functional Behavior Assessment for People with Autism** for more information.)*

Choose all that apply:

❑ Unstructured observation   ❑ Structured observation

❑ Interview   ❑ Descriptive analysis

❑ Hypothesis testing   ❑ Functional analysis

❑ Other _____

FUNCTION(S) OF THE BEHAVIOR:

Choose all that apply:

❑ Obtain attention   ❑ Escape/avoid something

❑ Obtain access to item/activity   ❑ Automatic reinforcement

❑ Special considerations _____

See special considerations discussed in Chapter 7.

SECTION 2: ANTECEDENT-BASED STRATEGIES

ANY IDENTIFIED SETTING EVENTS:
Use setting event checklist (Appendix).

PLANNED RESPONSES TO SETTING EVENTS:
Use suggestions from Chapter 3.

MOTIVATIVE INTERVENTIONS:
Decrease MO, create AO for response. (See Chapter 3 for suggestions.)

OTHER ANTECEDENT INTERVENTIONS:
Consider changing discriminative stimuli. (See Chapter 3 for suggestions.)

SECTION 3: TEACHING FUNCTIONAL ALTERNATIVES

REPLACEMENT SKILLS:
Use suggestions from Chapter 4.

SECTION 4: CONSEQUENCE-BASED INTERVENTIONS
Only use the sections below that apply to your child, student, or client.

REINFORCEMENT BASED STRATEGIES:
Consider various differential reinforcement schedules, discussed in Chapter 4 (DRI, DRA, DRH) and Chapter 5 (DRL, DRO).

EXTINCTION-BASED STRATEGIES:
Specify if a behavior will cease to be reinforced. Specify how (e.g., Do not provide a Cheez-It within 2 minutes of Joey yelling, "Cheez-It!")

PUNISHMENT-BASED STRATEGIES:
Consider both positive and negative strategies discussed in Chapter 5, if needed.

SECTION 5: KEEPING THE PLAN ON TRACK

CRITERIA FOR REEVALUATING PLAN:
Set a time period after which you will reevaluate the plan if there is either an increase in the problem behavior or insufficient decrease in the problem behavior.

CRITERIA FOR FADING PLAN:
Set goals for how long an individual should maintain a certain, lowered level of the problem behavior before the plan can be faded to a less intrusive level. Be sure to include specific steps for fading and criteria for returning to a more intrusive level.

CRITERIA FOR MASTERY:
Set a behavioral criteria after which the plan will be considered no longer necessary.

CRISIS INTEVENTION STRATEGIES:
If necessary, describe what to do if the behavior becomes dangerous. See discussion of unexpected dangerous behaviors in Chapter 10.

ATTACH YOUR GRAPH FOR THE BEHAVIOR PLAN
The assessment and baseline data graph can be used after you add a phase change line to indicate that the intervention has begun.

Attach graph of behavior plan.

10 | Frequently Asked Questions

1. What should you do if the behavior intervention plan works for a while, but then the problem behavior comes back?

This pattern likely suggests one of three problems. The first possibility is "procedural drift." This term refers to the tendency for people to deviate from an established plan over time. In other words, people start off administering the plan exactly to the letter, but over time, they slowly get more relaxed with it. This is a particular risk when intervening with problem behaviors, because once the behavior improves, the intervention team may lose their sense of urgency in implementing the plan. Other squeaky wheels get the grease while the problem behavior slowly creeps up again. The fading criteria are there for a reason. Help the team stick to them.

A second possible cause might be reinforcer substitution. As explained in Chapter 7, this means that the individual's problem behavior is no longer being reinforced by the factors/function you originally identified through an FBA, but by something else. For example, a behavior that was originally maintained by automatic reinforcement might become reinforced by access to a preferred activity if the individual is repeatedly redirected to this activity when she engages in the self-stimulatory behavior. Assess the treatment integrity. If, in fact, the plan is being implemented as intended, evaluate whether a new reinforcer for the problem behavior has emerged.

Finally, evaluate whether the plan may have relied too heavily on one reinforcer. For example, perhaps you developed a plan designed to treat a behavior problem that your child or student used to obtain potato chips. If chips are always used as a reinforcer, your child may satiate on chips over time. In other words, she might eventually get sick of the reinforcer. If that occurs, simply introduce an alternative reinforcer.

You can also try to avoid this problem by allowing for changes in your child's or student's MO while writing the plan. That is, be aware of how often the reinforcer will be provided and whether or not it would be better to offer a variety of reinforcers that all serve the same function. In the example above, offering a variety of snacks or drinks might be more effective than using chips every time.

2. What if the plan works in some situations, but not others (e.g., it works in reading class but not art class)?

In this case, evaluate both settings very carefully. The likelihood is that the plan is being implemented differently in one setting than another. Check the treatment integrity in each setting. If you do not detect any differences, then examine the problematic setting carefully with an eye toward identifying possible discriminative stimuli (situations that trigger the problem behavior). There must be a cue in this setting that was overlooked during the functional assessment.

3. What if the plan works, but a new problem behavior develops?

If a new problem behavior develops as the original behavior is decreasing, it probably means two things:
- the consequences in your plan were sufficiently meaningful to change the individual's behavior, but
- the function of the original problem behavior is not being met in an alternative fashion.

In other words, the individual's motivation to obtain whatever she was getting from the original problem behavior remains and the discriminative stimuli are still there, but the individual has no effective way to get what she wants. The new problem behavior is likely the individual's next attempt to get what she wants. For example, if a child who has been screaming in order to get candy in the checkout line at the grocery store discovers that this is no longer effective, she may throw herself on the floor and cry instead.

You should be able to solve the new behavior problem, if you:

- address antecedents (alter events that precede and may bring about the problem behavior), and
- teach replacement skills (provide new ways for the individual to get the things that she wants)

However, be sure to complete a functional assessment anyway, as the new behavior problem could have arisen coincidentally as well.

4. How do you request a functional behavior assessment and behavior plan from an educational agency (e.g., school, group home, day program, etc.)? How do you know they are conducting it properly?

To request an FBA, you must be familiar with the agency's system. Start by asking the direct care provider (e.g., teacher, home-based instructor, job coach) whom to contact to set up an FBA. Then, ask that person who will actually be conducting your child's or student's assessment.

Ideally, the person conducting the assessment will either be a Board Certified Behavior Analyst (BCBA), or will be supervised by one (see www.BACB.com for more information on certification). If the person you were referred to is not a BCBA or is not working with one, ask about his or her training in conducting FBAs. (This is a good question to ask even if the person is a BCBA.)

At a minimum, this person should have completed numerous FBAs with supervision. Ideally, she will have also completed multiple FBAs independently. Unfortunately, I have seen things described as FBAs that were no more than baseline data collection or educational recommendations. Ask the individual to describe the specific procedures that he or she has used to identify the functions of problem behaviors in the past. You will be able to tell from her answer whether she actually understands the FBA process. If you are not satisfied, request another consultant. When working with an agency, share your concerns with a supervisor. Bring this book along if you think it might be helpful to explain exactly what you want. If you are paying for the FBA yourself, you can probably find a good practitioner on the Behavior Analyst Certification Board website (www.BACB.com).

Next, ask the person how the FBA will be conducted. Every FBA should include observation, interview, and some descriptive analysis or structured observation. The person conducting the FBA should be willing to explain when and where your child or student will be observed, who he or she will interview, and how long the process will last. In addition, he or she should clearly explain your role in the process, and encourage your participation.

Once the FBA has been completed, it should include persuasive empirical evidence (data) that the identified function is actually controlling your child's or student's problem behavior. You should ask to see that data. The data should document multiple instances when the individual used the problem behavior for a particular purpose. It is not enough for the behavior to have been observed only once or twice. Furthermore, it is not enough for the FBA to be based on people's past recollections or assumptions about your child's or student's behavior.

Additionally, every FBA should be written up, even if the write-up is informal. If an FBA is conducted for your child, you should absolutely be given a copy of this report. If you are in any primary caregiving or educational role (e.g., teacher or adult service provider), you should also be given a copy of this report.

5. What if a parent or teacher will not follow through on an intervention that you have designed?

Once you have the behavior plan in hand, the tough task of behavior change begins. However, the person whose behavior you must begin to change is not the individual with autism. Rather, it is the people who care for her who must change their behavior. Even if you are one of those people, it may be a tough job. A behavior plan largely dictates environmental changes. That means the burden is on us to do the hard work. The problem behavior will simply disappear as a result. Of course, no one can guarantee that teachers, parents, therapists, or other independent adults will follow the recommendations of another adult. Nevertheless, there are strategies that will make it more likely that people will stick to the behavior plan:

a. *Include the people you will be asking to intervene with the behavior from the beginning of the assessment process.* They will be more likely to follow through if they feel invested in the behavior plan, and have had a say in what is and is not realistic to implement. Many parents have told me tales of crazed behavior analysts insisting that they implement programs at five-minute intervals throughout the day, never mind that they have a part-time job and two other children who need them. Although behavior intervention plans may represent the gold standard on paper, they are substandard if they are not sensible and realistic to implement. Listen to your team if they say your ideas are too challenging to implement. There is always another way to accomplish the same goal that might be more workable in any given setting. Remember, the best plan is the one that will actually be implemented.

b. *Invest some time training the team how to implement the behavior plan that you have created.* Many times, team members are too shy to say that they do not understand something. If you help them learn the plan, they will be more likely to implement it.

c. *Include a treatment integrity assessment form.* Assign someone to complete this form periodically. See the example in Chapter 8.

d. *Be sure the team sees the link between implementing the plan and reducing the individual's problem behavior.* This is often a big motivator. Highlight how much easier their jobs will be when the problem behavior is gone.

e. *Appreciate the team.* Thank them, point out gains you have seen, bake them cookies if you have to. Do what it takes to reward the team members for following the plan. (Remember, reinforcement increases appropriate behavior from everyone, not just people with autism!)

f. *Make things easy for the team.* While it may not be your job to make materials, purchase reinforcers, hang up visual cues, etc., if you reduce the effort required to implement the plan, it is more likely to get implemented. As a consultant, for example, I often do things that are not technically my job to ensure that they get done. I have cleaned and organized classrooms, updated weeks of graphs, moved furniture—whatever it takes. Typically, educational personnel and parents alike are working very hard. Anything you can do to help will increase the likelihood that your behavior intervention plan will get done.

g. The toughest situation to overcome is when a problem behavior may lead to a student's expulsion from a particular setting. As horrible a truth as it is, it may sometimes be more reinforcing for teachers to encourage the student's challenging behavior and ultimately get her out of the class than to actually solve the problem. If you ever suspect this is the situation, try to discuss your feelings with higher-ups. Persuade them to give the message that the student is staying in the class regardless of the outcome of this plan—even if it is not true! This will hopefully encourage staff members to give it their best effort.

6. What if you have a private FBA done and the agency serving your loved one won't implement the suggested interventions?

Unfortunately, it is not uncommon, due to philosophical differences, turf-related stand-offs, or defensiveness, for a school or agency to resist implementing suggestions arising from an FBA. If the plan has already been presented, you have taken every precaution to work with the provider, and there is still no follow-through, it often helps to be direct in addressing this.

Start by reserving judgment. Ask what the obstacles to implementing the plan are and suggest that you try to work together to identify strategies to overcome these. Perhaps the barriers are philosophical (e.g., "I'm not going to make a big deal and give him so much attention for doing what he should have done in the first place." Or, "if I did what you are asking me to, she'd be on break all day!"). If so, try to explain the plan in language the individual will find more palatable. For example: "You are really giving him the same level of attention as you are giving the other students, it's just that he has autism and needs the attention exaggerated to perceive it." Or, "Believe me, I don't want him getting extra attention any more than you do, but this is less attention than he is getting for the problem behavior so we are actually taking attention away."

If you are a parent or guardian, you may not even be given an opportunity to speak to the frontline providers about their resistance to implementing the behavior plan. You must speak with a supervisor. Ask for treatment integrity data right away. If you are still encountering resistance, refer to the Individuals with Disabilities Education

Act (IDEA 2004), which specifies that a functional assessment must be implemented.

It is also wise for parents to plan ahead to ensure continued implementation of a behavior intervention plan. For example, if your child's teacher will be taking an extended absence (e.g., a maternity leave), speak to the supervisor about training the substitute teacher. Post the intervention (without last names) in the classroom in case the teacher is absent due to illness. And if you need to go away for a business trip or a weekend, make sure that whoever will be watching your child at home practices the intervention plan under your supervision before you leave.

7. What if an individual's behavior is related to the behavior of a sibling or another student in a class?

It is not uncommon for one individual's problem behavior to set off another individual's problem behavior. A classic example of this is a classroom in which one student's problem behavior is screaming, and the other's problem behavior is her response to loud noises. While this kind of chain reaction is obviously frustrating and stressful to deal with, an alternate way of looking at this is that the person whose behaviors are getting set off is actually benefiting from multiple practice opportunities to use her replacement behavior. In reality, the MO for engaging in the problem behavior will occur in many settings. Both people with problem behaviors need to have FBAs and behavior plans. In the event that the first person's behavior sets off a dangerous or destructive behavior in the second person, it may be best to separate the individuals, if possible.

8. What if a child's behavior is reinforced by a peer, classmate, or sibling? What if someone is intentionally provoking the problem behavior?

Sometimes, an individual's behavior is reinforced, intentionally or unintentionally, by peers. Classmates laugh at wisecracks, encourage classroom disruptions, or hand each other things that may have been asked for inappropriately. Siblings try to get one another in trouble, or may get one another to do a problem behavior as a type of teasing or bullying. In these cases, the peers must be held accountable.

Peers must be trained in how to respond appropriately, and contingencies must be set in place to make sure that they do. For example, a classmate who encourages classroom disruptions might be given detention; a sibling who tricks her sister into embarrassing herself in public might be forced to make a public apology.

This strategy only applies to instances where the peers are responding favorably to the challenging behavior. If peers are actually responding with fear or unhappiness to a behavior, they cannot be held accountable for their responses. For example, one student I work with repeatedly stole the football from a group of boys playing at recess. He was reinforced by their attention (although it was very negative), yet it would have been unfair, if not impossible, to ask the boys not to roll their eyes and complain at the loss of their ball. Instead, the student with autism was taught to solicit attention at recess from a different group of boys who would be more likely to react favorably to an appropriate initiation. He was also taught to recognize nonverbal cues that other children were receptive to interacting with him at a given time.

Other students I have worked with have actually scared, injured, or seriously upset their peers. These children were taught to recognize precursors to the problem behavior to avoid injury, or were taught not to be afraid of the unfamiliar behavior, where appropriate. Another strategy is to introduce and reinforce appropriate alternative behaviors for the student with the problem behavior. For example, Riley, the student mentioned in Chapter 7 who threw chairs to get attention, was taught to tell jokes and read stories to kindergartners to get attention instead.

9. What should you do in response to an unexpected challenging behavior?

Some problem behaviors make you say, "Where did that come from?" Maybe these behaviors are part of an emerging pattern—there has to be a first time for everything. Alternatively, these occurrences might be part of a pattern of very low frequency behaviors. Finally, they may be occurrences of behaviors that you thought were gone. In any case, some behaviors catch people off guard.

Mild Behaviors: Some behavioral surprises do not place any people or property in danger. These may be mildly annoying or interfering behaviors. Some examples might include the sudden appearance of a lisp, hand-flapping, or self-talk. For these behaviors, the safest bet is to act as if they never happened. Ideally, the environment should remain unchanged. Most likely, the occurrence of the behavior was random. If it is not reinforced, it will not recur. Any response, even a startled face or a reprimand, might inadvertently act as a reinforcer. When the people in the environment do not respond to a behavior, it takes the power out of that behavior. It is like removing the behavior's batteries. This approach works best for a new behavior because no reinforcement pattern has been established. Once a pattern has been established, ceasing to respond to an individual's behavior is actually an intervention, as the consequence will now be changed. No intervention should take place until after a functional behavior assessment has been completed. If a behavior occurs more than a few times, it makes sense to begin completing an FBA.

The one situation in which initially turning a blind eye toward a behavior will *not* prevent future recurrence is when a behavior is maintained by automatic reinforcement. For example, if a child with autism is running back and forth along a fence because it provides a pleasant internal sensation, then ignoring the behavior will probably not decrease it in any way. In that situation, environmental change, or the lack of change, will have no impact on the behavior.

Dangerous Behaviors: Other unexpected behaviors are, in fact, dangerous. To preserve the safety of people and property around the individual, a response is warranted. In those cases, begin assessment right away. One occurrence of a dangerous behavior is enough to merit the time and resources of an assessment team.

For low frequency, high intensity behaviors, gathering interview data may be the best that you can do to start. After all, if you have only seen the behavior once and you don't know what set it off, it may be difficult to plan an observation of it. However, it may be enough to put some antecedent strategies in place to prevent future injury or loss. That is, you guess at the function of the behavior and make sure the person is given access to everything she might have been trying to obtain with the behavior while additional information can be collected. This should preserve safety and give you time to implement a longer-term intervention.

In the meantime, you will have to do something in the moment that the dangerous behavior is occurring. Because safety is always the first priority in behavioral intervention, use a "crisis management" approach. To summarize, "crisis management" means keep everybody safe, at all costs. That means that even if you risk reinforcing a problem behavior, you must do what you need to do to end the dangerous behavior in the moment.

For example, a student named Alexis pointed a pair of scissors menacingly at a teacher. The teacher had been ignoring Alexis's inappropriate wisecracks and other undesirable bids for attention. Brandishing the scissors was clearly an escalated bid for attention. The teacher wisely responded by asking Alexis to sit in her seat and talked with Alexis about what she could do instead next time. Although this immediate attention may have acted as a reinforcer, which might have implications for the future, the priority from a crisis management approach is to end the immediate danger. By providing the attention Alexis craved, the teacher minimized the chance of her escalating the behavior further. Threatening someone with scissors can be viewed as a request. Satisfying the request will end the problem behavior related to requesting. In this way, the threatening situation with the scissors was ended by reinforcing the problem behavior.

There are also other helpful strategies for crisis management:

- Keep other people away from the person who is engaging in the dangerous behavior.
- If you can, move the person with the dangerous behavior away from others. However, if a behavior problem has escalated to dangerous levels, this may be easier said than done. If so, have bystanders leave the area where the individual is engaging in the dangerous behavior.
- Also remove possibly dangerous items from the area (e.g., scissors, pens, etc.).

To accomplish these objectives, you may need help. Anyone who works with individuals with autism and related disorders should have a system in place that enables them to call for backup. Consider using a cell phone system or intercom, sending a reliable student for assistance, etc.

Finally, everyone who works with or cares for someone with autism should seek out crisis management training. This will be especially helpful for parents or group home staff who may not always have a backup person to call for help. Your state developmental disabilities agency may be able to help you locate appropriate training.

10. To what extent should the person with the behavior problem be involved in developing and implementing the behavior plan?

Some individuals with autism and related disorders are capable of participating in the development of their own behavior plan. To the maximum of their ability to respond to abstract questions such as, "When are you least likely to do the behavior?" or "Why do you think you do that?", you should involve the individual in creating the plan.

First of all, your child or student probably knows herself better than the intervention team does. Second of all, she is more likely to actively participate and celebrate her success in the plan if she has had a say in the plan.

For example, my colleague currently works with a high school student with Asperger's disorder who is earning money toward going out to lunch for doing as he is asked and refraining from outbursts in his classes. They recently tweaked the system slightly so that he was earning tokens representing money rather than actual money. His behavior worsened. His consultant asked him what was going on, and he explained that he had been more excited to earn real money. They reinstated the original system and his behavior improved.

For any behavior plan, making the student explicitly aware of the consequences for each behavior can speed up behavior change. This way she will not have to repeatedly experience the contingencies to learn them. Instead, the individual can learn the contingencies simply by being told. Depending on the individual, you may want to talk to her about the consequences before the behavior, after the behavior, or both. For example, when you are first implementing the behavior plan, you can explain briefly what reinforcement she will receive for doing the desired behavior. For example, "You will get a break if you follow Mrs. Harper's directions without flopping on the floor." Then, after she has received the reinforcer, you can link the reinforcer to her actions. For example, "See how quickly you get your break when you follow directions!"

11 | The Top Ten Strategies to Prevent Challenging Behavior

It's always better to prevent challenging behaviors than to react to them. While a functionally based behavior intervention plan will be effective, it will require time and attention, both of which are usually in short supply! Also, challenging behaviors cause distress for the individual who is engaging in them, as well as for those around him. In sum, as with all things, an ounce of prevention is worth a pound of cure.

The following strategies are designed to prevent a variety of challenging behaviors. They address common motivators with the idea that if an individual's needs in these realms are met, then he will not develop problem behaviors in the first place. These strategies are reminiscent of those you might come across through a school-wide positive behavioral support program (see www.PBIS.org). Routinely incorporating these strategies will prevent a large percentage of behavior problems, and allow you to devote precious time and resources to the fewer problems that do develop.

1. Offer choices.

Throughout the day, during school, work, and leisure activities, let the individual with autism make his own choices whenever possible. Consider offering options for meals, for the order of completing tasks, for the order of completing leisure activities, for types of tasks and activities, for clothes to wear, etc. Even if the choices your child or student makes are not optimal, allow him to make his own choices, as long as they are not harmful. Making choices improves quality of life, which in turn decreases the chance for problem behaviors.

2. Follow the individual's lead.

In larger issues as well as day-to-day issues, follow the individual's lead. For example, when selecting a job site for an adult with autism, look for a job that matches his interests and abilities, rather than just settling for a job that is easy to obtain. Ensure that someone who likes to interact with others does not get a job working alone in a stockroom, or that a bright adult with autism who has a low tolerance for boredom is not asked to work in an assembly line. Similarly, when looking for a supervised apartment for an adult who hates noise, stay away from buildings close to busy streets. Or, if an individual with autism is not interested in socializing, do not try to force him into friendships. Have a realistic sense of whether the choices that you are making are in the best interest of the individual with autism, rather than your own best interest.

3. Keep it simple.

Make things as easy on the individual with autism as possible. Break tasks down into simpler parts, use visual cues, and organize school, work, and living spaces. By doing this, you will remove obstacles from his day-to-day success, thereby reducing the likelihood of challenging behaviors. Also keep it simple for family members and staff. Only intervene with a problem behavior when necessary (see Chapter 1). Keep plans simple. This will allow you to conserve resources for when they are absolutely needed.

4. Pay lots of positive attention to the individual with autism.

When you pay attention to someone's appropriate, on-task behaviors, there is less risk that you will give him attention for inappropriate behaviors in the form of reprimands or redirection. You decrease the chances that you will pair yourself with negative attention, as your attention is more often paired with praise and positive interactions. You also decrease the risk that the person will use inappropriate behaviors to obtain your attention. Finally, making an effort to "catch the individual being good" counteracts the tendency to focus on disabilities and what the person has trouble doing rather than on his abilities and what he does well.

5. Provide plenty of access to preferred items.

When people with autism have enriched environments, it decreases the risk that they will engage in behaviors that are maintained by automatic reinforcement. Automatic reinforcement behaviors, such as repetitive movements that occur solely because they feel good, are essentially a way of filling time or entertaining oneself. It is like singing in the car, or doodling during a boring lecture. If someone is already entertained, he will have less need for automatic reinforcement.

If you are not sure what items or activities your child or student prefers, consider letting him sample many different types of items and activities and take note of which things he spends more time with or seems more interested in. Try to identify at least two or three types of foods, drinks, sensations, motor activities, manipulatives, etc. so that a variety of options are available.

6. Keep work interesting.

If tasks are at an appropriately challenging level and taught in a meaningful way, your child or student is likely to find the activities engaging and rewarding. This will prevent him from using behaviors aimed at escaping the tasks, as well as automatic reinforcement behaviors that may stem from being bored. Furthermore, a stimulating school or work environment improves quality of life, which, again, decreases the risk of challenging behaviors.

7. Keep days interesting.

It can be challenging to fill the time for some individuals with autism. Cognitive, social, and other challenges may limit the independent leisure activities they are able to do. You can help prevent challenging behaviors by ensuring that the person has a structured, full day. Keeping him occupied with interesting activities helps him know what *to* do, not just what *not* to do.

8. Build strong communication skills.

As explained in earlier chapters in the book, most challenging behaviors occur when people don't have any other effective way of communicating their wants and needs. If someone has a strong communicative repertoire, he no longer needs to use inappropriate behaviors to make requests. While your child or student is learning to communicate more appropriately, it is vital to reinforce his appropriate attempts at communicating. Prioritize building his communication skills above all other goals.

9. Pick your battles.

If you do not need to intervene with a behavior, don't. There will be plenty of opportunities to use your resources for teaching skills and addressing other problem behaviors. If the person's behavior is not interfering with his everyday functioning, leave it alone. Keep it simple.

10. Respect the individual's right to be himself.

People who have autism and related disorders may have unusual likes and dislikes, as well as unusual habits. These idiosyncrasies are not necessarily undesirable, just unusual. Some of these behaviors are only problems because we see them that way. Alternatively, we could try to accept aspects of the individual that are not actually interfering with his daily life. We could think of some of these things as "quirky" rather than as problem behaviors. For example, unless it is causing teasing or some other negative outcome, maybe hand-flapping could be considered your child's way of showing excitement. Jumping or touching surfaces could be considered in the same ballpark as the behaviors of your idiosyncratic uncle who tells the same jokes at every family function.

If you respect your child's or student's differences, he will feel your respect. This will decrease your stress and the perception of power struggles on both sides.

Most likely, you sometimes permit yourself to wear clothes that don't match, lie on the couch all day, eat too much junk food, or do other things that others might consider "bad." This kind of permission to sometimes just be yourself can be helpful for individuals with autism too. Although you are now armed with an arsenal full of behavior change tools, don't feel that you always need to use them.

Appendices

Appendix A
Setting Events Checklist

Sample—Completed Setting Events Checklist
sent from Home to School

Sample—Completed Setting Events Checklist
sent from School to Home

Appendix B
Behavior Intervention Plan Protocol Form

Sample—Completed Behavior Intervention Plan Protocol Form

SETTING EVENTS CHECKLIST

Child/Client: _____ Date: _____

Person reporting: _____

Period of time being described: _____

To the best of your knowledge, please record whether or not any of the events below occurred while _____ was in your care.

Health Issues

- ❏ Less sleep than usual
- ❏ More sleep than usual
- ❏ Ate less than usual
- ❏ Ate more than usual
- ❏ Drank less than usual
- ❏ Drank more than usual
- ❏ Urinated less than usual
- ❏ Urinated more than usual
- ❏ Had fewer bowel movements than usual
- ❏ Had more bowel movements than usual
- ❏ Appears less active than usual
- ❏ Appears more active than usual
- ❏ Medication has been changed/missed
- ❏ Has menstrual period
- ❏ Has engaged in masturbation/attempts more than usual
- ❏ Has been sneezing or had runny nose
- ❏ Has vomited
- ❏ Has had rash
- ❏ Has had temperature above 99.5
- ❏ Has had other signs of illness or allergy
- ❏ Had a seizure

Other possible stressors

- ❏ Schedule was unexpectedly changed
- ❏ Preferred food items were not available
- ❏ Preferred activities were not available
- ❏ Preferred people were not available
- ❏ Witnessed another person in distress
- ❏ Witnessed another person being reprimanded
- ❏ Witnessed an argument
- ❏ Was injured
- ❏ Was reprimanded
- ❏ Was in an argument
- ❏ Was bullied or teased
- ❏ An expected desired event did not occur
- ❏ Was in a crowd more than usual
- ❏ Was alone more than usual
- ❏ Was unusually rushed
- ❏ Was excluded from social interaction

Sample Completed

SETTING EVENTS CHECKLIST
Sent from Home to School

(Note: Given that Grace's aggressions function to obtain peer attention and are more likely to occur after witnessing an argument between her parents, the fact that a preferred person was unavailable this morning and she witnessed an argument might strengthen her MO for social attention, and therefore might make aggression more likely.)

Child/Client: ___Grace Carmichael___ Date: _5/6/08_

Person reporting: ___Mother___

Period of time being described: ___Last night — this morning___

To the best of your knowledge, please record whether or not any of the events below occurred while ___Grace___ was in your care.

Health Issues

- ❏ Less sleep than usual
- ❏ More sleep than usual
- ❏ Ate less than usual
- ❏ Ate more than usual
- ❏ Drank less than usual
- ❏ Drank more than usual
- ❏ Urinated less than usual
- ❏ Urinated more than usual
- ❏ Had fewer bowel movements than usual
- ❏ Had more bowel movements than usual
- ❏ Appears less active than usual
- ❏ Appears more active than usual
- ❏ Medication has been changed/missed
- ❏ Has menstrual period
- ❏ Has engaged in masturbation/attempts more than usual
- ❏ Has been sneezing or had runny nose
- ❏ Has vomited
- ❏ Has had rash
- ❏ Has had temperature above 99.5
- ❏ Has had other signs of illness or allergy
- ❏ Had a seizure

Other possible stressors

- ☒ Schedule was unexpectedly changed
- ☐ Preferred food items were not available
- ☐ Preferred activities were not available
- ☒ Preferred people were not available
- ☐ Witnessed another person in distress
- ☐ Witnessed another person being reprimanded
- ☒ Witnessed an argument
- ☐ Was injured
- ☐ Was reprimanded
- ☐ Was in an argument
- ☐ Was bullied or teased
- ☐ An expected desired event did not occur
- ☐ Was in a crowd more than usual
- ☐ Was alone more than usual
- ☒ Was unusually rushed
- ☐ Was excluded from social interaction

Sample Completed
SETTING EVENTS CHECKLIST
Sent from School to Home

(Note: Given the function of Grace's aggressions, a problem behavior might be expected with the social exclusion described below.)

Child/Client: ___Grace Carmichael___ Date: _5/6/08_

Person reporting: ___Teacher___

Period of time being described: ___Today at school___

To the best of your knowledge, please record whether or not any of the events below occurred while ___Grace___ was in your care.

Health Issues

- ☐ Less sleep than usual
- ☐ More sleep than usual
- ☐ Ate less than usual
- ☐ Ate more than usual
- ☐ Drank less than usual
- ☐ Drank more than usual
- ☐ Urinated less than usual
- ☐ Urinated more than usual
- ☐ Had fewer bowel movements than usual
- ☐ Had more bowel movements than usual
- ☒ Appears less active than usual
- ☐ Appears more active than usual
- ☐ Medication has been changed/missed
- ☐ Has menstrual period
- ☐ Has engaged in masturbation/attempts more than usual
- ☒ Has been sneezing or had runny nose
- ☐ Has vomited
- ☐ Has had rash
- ☐ Has had temperature above 99.5
- ☐ Has had other signs of illness or allergy
- ☐ Had a seizure

Other possible stressors

- ☐ Schedule was unexpectedly changed
- ☐ Preferred food items were not available
- ☐ Preferred activities were not available
- ☒ Preferred people were not available
- ☐ Witnessed another person in distress
- ☐ Witnessed another person being reprimanded
- ☐ Witnessed an argument
- ☐ Was injured
- ☐ Was reprimanded
- ☐ Was in an argument
- ☐ Was bullied or teased
- ☐ An expected desired event did not occur
- ☐ Was in a crowd more than usual
- ☒ Was alone more than usual
- ☐ Was unusually rushed
- ☒ Was excluded from social interaction

BEHAVIOR INTERVENTION PLAN PROTOCOL FORM

SECTION 1: BACKGROUND AND FUNCTIONAL ASSESSMENT INFORMATION

NAME OF STUDENT/CLIENT:_____

INTERVENTION TEAM: _____

_____

_____

TEAM LEADER(S):_____

_____

_____

PROBLEM BEHAVIOR (S):_____

_____

_____

_____

_____

MEASUREMENT PLAN: _____

_____

_____

_____

_____

REASON FOR ADDRESSING BEHAVIOR:

Choose all that apply:

❏ Danger to self ❏ Danger to others

❏ Risk of property damage ❏ Stigmatizing

❏ Interferes with own adaptive behaviors

❏ Interferes with others' adaptive behaviors

❏ Other _____

FUNCTIONAL ASSESSMENT METHODS USED:

Choose all that apply:

❏ Unstructured observation ❏ Structured observation

❏ Interview ❏ Descriptive analysis

❏ Hypothesis testing ❏ Functional analysis

❏ Other _____

FUNCTION(S) OF THE BEHAVIOR:

Choose all that apply:

❏ Obtain attention ❏ Escape/avoid something

❏ Obtain access to item/activity ❏ Automatic reinforcement

❏ Special considerations _____

SECTION 2: ANTECEDENT-BASED STRATEGIES

ANY IDENTIFIED SETTING EVENTS:_____

_____

_____

_____

_____

PLANNED RESPONSES TO SETTING EVENTS:_____

_____

_____

_____

_____

MOTIVATIVE INTERVENTIONS: _____

_____

_____

_____

_____

OTHER ANTECEDENT INTERVENTIONS:_____

_____

_____

_____

_____

SECTION 3: TEACHING FUNCTIONAL ALTERNATIVES

REPLACEMENT SKILLS:_____

_____

_____

_____

_____

SECTION 4: CONSEQUENCE-BASED INTERVENTIONS
Only use the sections below that apply to your child, student, or client.

REINFORCEMENT-BASED STRATEGIES:_____

_____

_____

_____

EXTINCTION-BASED STRATEGIES:_____

_____

_____

_____

PUNISHMENT-BASED STRATEGIES:_____

_____

_____

_____

_____

SECTION 5: KEEPING THE PLAN ON TRACK

CRITERIA FOR REEVALUATING PLAN:_____

_____

_____

_____

CRITERIA FOR FADING PLAN:_____

_____

_____

_____

CRITERIA FOR MASTERY:_____

_____

_____

_____

CRISIS INTEVENTION STRATEGIES:_____

_____

_____

_____

Attach graph of behavior plan.

Sample Completed
BEHAVIOR INTERVENTION PLAN PROTOCOL FORM

SECTION 1: BACKGROUND AND FUNCTIONAL ASSESSMENT INFORMATION

NAME OF STUDENT/CLIENT: Grace Carmichael

INTERVENTION TEAM: Regular education teacher, special education teacher, behavior consultant, parents

TEAM LEADER(S): Special education teacher

PROBLEM BEHAVIOR (S): Causing injury to peers via hitting or biting, either with a hand or an object

MEASUREMENT PLAN: Frequency of each of 2 levels of aggressive acts per hour: 1) leaves no mark, bruise, or blood; 2) leaves a mark or bruise or draws blood

REASON FOR ADDRESSING BEHAVIOR:

Choose all that apply:

- ☐ Danger to self
- ☒ Danger to others
- ☒ Risk of property damage
- ☒ Stigmatizing
- ☒ Interferes with own adaptive behaviors
- ☒ Interferes with others' adaptive behaviors
- ☐ Other _____

FUNCTIONAL ASSESSMENT METHODS USED:

Choose all that apply:

- ☒ Unstructured observation
- ☒ Structured observation
- ☒ Interview
- ☒ Descriptive analysis
- ☒ Hypothesis testing
- ☐ Functional analysis
- ☐ Other _____

FUNCTION(S) OF THE BEHAVIOR:

Choose all that apply:

- ☒ Obtain attention
- ☐ Escape/avoid something
- ☐ Obtain access to item/activity
- ☐ Automatic reinforcement
- ☒ Special considerations ___Behavior maintained by peer attention only___

SECTION 2: ANTECEDENT-BASED STRATEGIES

ANY IDENTIFIED SETTING EVENTS: • Exclusion by peers

• Witnessing an argument

PLANNED RESPONSES TO SETTING EVENTS: • Split class into pairs for a project to ensure Grace has access to peer attention.

• Assign Grace and a partner to walk attendance list to the main office together to allow for some antecedent peer interaction.

• Offer a "lunch bunch" to ensure peer attention at lunch.

• Offer an organized activity at recess to ensure peer attention.

• At home, if a peer buddy is not available for an activity, skip the activity.

MOTIVATIVE INTERVENTIONS: • Playgroups with peers will be arranged for 2 afternoons per week. Grace will be matched with a peer buddy to arrange activities after school.

• Scheduled attention from peer buddies at half-hour intervals (peers will be trained and sign up on a sign-up sheet).

• Peers will be prompted to respond to Grace if she has had 3 unsuccessful initiations.

• If Grace will be in a group of peers who are unlikely to reinforce her initiations, a preferred activity will be offered to her in a different area where she will be separated from the non-responsive peers.

OTHER ANTECEDENT INTERVENTIONS: none

SECTION 3: TEACHING FUNCTIONAL ALTERNATIVES

REPLACEMENT SKILLS: • Social skills training to take place during twice weekly, school-based buddy skills group focusing on: initiating to peers, reinforcement peer initiations, interpreting peer facial expressions, interpreting peer tone of voice, maintaining peer initiations. • Parent training regarding carrying over social skills practice to the home and community.

SECTION 4: CONSEQUENCE-BASED INTERVENTIONS
Only use the sections below that apply to your child, student, or client.

REINFORCEMENT-BASED STRATEGIES: • Peers will be trained to reinforce appropriate initiations made by Grace.

• Grace will be allowed to participate in an after-school peer interaction if she has been gentle with peers during the shool day.

• Grace will be allowed to call her cousin and say goodnight if she has been gentle during after school peer activities.

EXTINCTION-BASED STRATEGIES: • Peers will be trained not to speak to Grace about her aggressions.

PUNISHMENT-BASED STRATEGIES: none

SECTION 5: KEEPING THE PLAN ON TRACK

CRITERIA FOR REEVALUATING PLAN: • Failure to show reduction in problem behavior after one week.

CRITERIA FOR FADING PLAN: • Zero levels of the problem behavior for three consecutive weeks. Increase scheduled peer attention in school by 5-minute intervals each time this milestone is missed.

CRITERIA FOR MASTERY: • Zero levels of the problem behavior for six consecutive months.

CRISIS INTEVENTION STRATEGIES: • Keep Grace away from peers for the remainder of the school day (or afternoon if at home) if she attempts an aggressive act.

Attach graph of behavior plan.

References

Austin, J., Weatherly, N. L., & Gravina, N. E. (2005). Using task clarification, graphic feedback, and verbal feedback to increase closing-task completion in a privately owned restaurant. *Journal of Applied Behavior Analysis, 38,* 117-20.

Bolstad, O. D., & Johnson, S. M. (1972). Self-regulation in the modification of disruptive classroom behavior. *Journal of Applied Behavior Analysis, 5,* 443-54.

Bondy, A., & Frost, L. (2002). *The Picture Exchange Communication System.* Newark, DE: Pyramid Educational Products.

Carr, E. G., & Durand, V. M. (1985). Reducing behavior problems through functional communication training. *Journal of Applied Behavior Analysis, 18,* 111-26.

Carr, E. G., Horner, R. H., Turnbull, A. P., Marquis, J. G., Magito-McLaughlin, D., McAtee, M. L., Smith, C. E., & Ryan, K. A., Ruef, M. B., & Doolabh, A. (1999). *Positive behavior support as an approach for dealing with problem behavior in people with developmental disabilities: A research synthesis.* American Association on Mental Retardation Monograph Series.

Catania, A. C. (1998). *Learning.* Upper Saddle River, NJ: Simon & Schuster.

Cooper, J. O., Heron, T. E., & Heward, W. L. (2007). *Applied Behavior Analysis.* Upper Saddle River, NJ: Pearson Education, Inc.

Delmolino, L., & Harris, S. (2004). *Incentives for Change: Motivating People with Autism Spectrum Disorders to Learn and Gain Independence.* Bethesda, MD: Woodbine House.

Dozier, C. L., Vollmer, T. R., Borrero, J. C., Borrero, C. S., Rapp, J. T., Bourret, J., & Guitterez, A. (2007). Assessment of preference for behavioral treatment versus baseline conditions. *Behavioral Interventions, 22,* 245-61.

Durand, V. M., & Crimmins, D. B. (1988). Identifying variables maintaining self-injurious behavior. *Journal of Autism and Developmental Disabilities, 18,* 99-117.

Ervin, R. A., DuPaul, G. J., Kern, L., & Friman, P. C. (1998). Classroom-based functional and adjunctive assessments: Proactive approaches to intervention selection for adolescents with attention deficit hyperactivity disorder. *Journal of Applied Behavior Analysis, 31,* 65-78.

Ferster, C. B. (1958). Control of behavior in chimpanzees and pigeons by time out from positive reinforcement. *Psychological Monographs, 72,* 108.

Frea, W. D., & Hughes, C. (1997). Functional analysis and treatment of social-communicative behavior of adolescents with developmental disabilities. *Journal of Applied Behavior Analysis, 30,* 701-704.

Glasberg, B. (2005). *Functional Behavior Assessment for People with Autism: Making Sense of Seemingly Senseless Behavior.* Bethesda, MD: Woodbine House.

Hanley, G. P., Piazza, C. C., Fisher, W. W., & Maglieri, K. A. (2005). On the effectiveness of and preference for punishment and extinction components of function-based interventions. *Journal of Applied Behavior Analysis, 38,* 51-65.

Herrnstein, R. J. (1970). On the law of effect. *Journal of the Experimental Analysis of Behavior,* 13, 243-266.

Hoch, H., McComas, J. J., Johnson, L., Faranda, N., & Guenther, S. L. (2002). The effects of magnitude and quality of reinforcement on choice responding during play activities. *Journal of Applied Behavior Analysis,* 35, 171-81.

Horner, R.H., & Sugai, G., (2005). School-wide positive behavior support: An alternative approach to discipline in schools. (pp. 359-90). In L. Bambara & L. Kern (Eds.), *Positive Behavior Support.* New York, NY: Guilford Press.

Individuals with Disabilities Education Act Amendments of 2004, 20 U.S.C. 1401-1485.

Iwata, B. A., Dorsey, M. F., Slifer, K. J., Bauman. K. E., & Richman, G. S. (1982). Toward a functional analysis of self-injury. *Analysis and Intervention in Developmental Disabilities, 2,* 3-20.

Iwata, B. A., Pace, G. M., Cowdery, G. E., & Miltenberger, R. G. (1994). What makes extinction work: An analysis of procedural form and function. *Journal of Applied Behavior Analysis,* 27, 131-44.

Iwata, B. A., Pace, G. M., Dorsey, M. F., Zarcone, J. R., Vollmer, T. R., Smith, R. G., Rodgers, T. A., Lerman, D. C., Shore, B. A., Mazaleski, J. L., Goh, H.-L., Cowdery, G. E., Kalsher, M. J., McCosh, K. C., & Willis, K. D. (1994). The functions of self-injurious behavior: An experimental-epidemiological analysis. *Journal of Applied Behavior Analysis, 27,* 215-40.

Kantor, J. R. (1959). *Interbehavioral Psychology.* Granville, OH: Principia Press.

Kern, L., Dunlap, G., Clarke, S., & Childs, K. (1994). Student-assisted functional assessment interview. *Diagnostique, 19 (2-3),* 29-39.

Kwak, M. M., Ervin, R. A., Anderson, M. Z., & Austin, J. (2004). Agreement of function across methods used in school-based functional assessment with preadolescent and adolescent students. *Behavior Modification, 28 (3),* 375-401.

Laraway, S., Snycerski, S., Michael, J., & Poling, A. (2001). The abative effect: A new term to describe the action of antecedents that reduce operant responding. *The Analysis of Verbal Behavior, 18,* 101-104.

Lerman, D. C., & Vorndran, C. M. (2002). On the status of knowledge for using punishment: Implications for treating behavior disorders. *Journal of Applied Behavior Analysis, 35,* 431-64.

Michael, J. (1982). Distinguishing between discriminative and motivational functions of stimuli. *Journal of the Experimental Analysis of Behavior, 37,* 149-55.

Mueller, M. M., Sterling-Turner, H. E., & Scattone, D. (2001). Functional assessment of hand flapping in a general education classroom. *Journal of Applied Behavior Analysis, 34,* 233-36.

Neef, N. A., & Peterson, S. M. (2007). Functional Behavior Assessment. In J. O. Cooper, T. E. Heron, & W. L. Heward (Eds.), *Applied Behavior Analysis* (pp. 500–524). Upper Saddle River, NJ: Pearson Education.

Ratner, S. C. (1970). Habituation: Research and theory. In J. H. Reynierse (Ed.), *Current Issues in Animal Learning* (pp. 55-84). Lincoln, NE: University of Nebraska Press.

Reed, H., Thomas, E., Sprague, J. R., & Horner, R. H. (1997). The student guided functional assessment interview: An analysis of student and teacher agreement. *Journal of Behavioral Education, 7 (1),* 33-49.

Repp, A. C., Felce, D., & Barton, L. E. (1988). Basing the treatment of stereotypic and self-injurious behaviors on hypotheses of their causes. *Journal of Applied Behavior Analysis, 21,* 281-89.

Romanowich, P., Bourret, J., & Vollmer, T. R. (2007). Further analysis of the matching law to describe two and three point shot allocation by professional basketball players. *Journal of Applied Behavior Analysis, 40,* 311-315.

Skinner, B. F. (1953). *Science and Human Behavior.* New York, NY: The Macmillan Company.

Skinner, B. F. (1984). The operational analysis of psychological terms. *Behavioral and Brain Sciences, 7,* 547-82.

Smith, S.W., & Farrell, D.T. (1993). Level system use in special education: Classroom intervention with prima facie appeal. *Behavior Disorders, 18,* 251-64

Smith, R. G., & Iwata, B. A. (1997). Antecedent influences on behavior disorders. *Journal of Applied Behavior Analysis, 30,* 343-75.

Sundberg, M. L., & Partington, J.W. (1998). *Teaching Language to Children with Autism or Other Developmental Disabilities.* Danville, CA: Behavior Analysts, Inc.

Tustin, R. D. (1994). Preference for reinforcers under varying schedule arrangements: A behavioral economic analysis. *Journal of Applied Behavior Analysis, 27,* 597-606.

Vollmer, T. R., & Iwata, B. A. (1991). Establishing operations and reinforcement effects. *Journal of Applied Behavior Analysis, 24,* 279-91.

White, O. R., & Haring, N. G. (1980). *Exceptional Teaching.* 2nd edition. Columbus, OH: Charles E. Merrill.

Index

Page numbers in *italics* indicate figures

About the Author

Beth A. Glasberg, Ph.D., BCBA, is the director of Glasberg Behavioral Consulting Services, LLC in Allentown, New Jersey. She is a Board Certified Behavior Analyst and two-time recipient of the Lebec Prize for Research in Autism. She is the author of *Functional Behavior Assessment for People with Autism* and the coauthor of *Siblings of Children with Autism*, both published by Woodbine House.